THE SPANISH TRAGEDY

Thomas Kyd

AUTHORED by Taro Kuriyama
UPDATED AND REVISED by Jordan Berkow

COVER DESIGN by Table XI Partners LLC
COVER PHOTO by Olivia Verma and © 2005 GradeSaver, LLC

BOOK DESIGN by Table XI Partners LLC

Published by GradeSaver LLC, www.gradesaver.com

First published in the United States of America by GradeSaver LLC. 2007

ISBN 978-1-60259-110-3

Printed in the United States of America

For other products and additional information please visit http://www.gradesaver.com

Table of Contents

Table of Contents

Biography of Thomas Kyd (1558-1594)

Thomas Kyd was born in 1558, six years before Shakespeare and Marlowe. Parish records indicate that he lived in London with his parents and two other siblings-of which one died in 1602. His father, Francis Kyd, was a scrivener. Eminent biographer Arthur Freeman observes that while scriveners garnered little respect from contemporary writers, they profited considerably from their monopoly on many official documents. Francis Kyd's official title read "Writer of the Court Letter" (3). As a member of a comfortable middle-class household, Thomas was enrolled in the Merchant Taylors' School at the age of seven.

As opposed to St. Paul's or Eton, Merchant Taylors' was a decidedly middle-class school. Nevertheless, even the admission requirements speak to the school's educational capabilities: as Freeman notes, the young Kyd was required to know the "the catechism in English or Latyn," and be able to "read perfectly & write competently" (6). No records indicate how long Kyd remained at Merchant Taylors' School, nor are there any records that indicate that he matriculated in Oxford or Cambridge, as did his schoolmate and predecessor Edmund Spenser (1552-1599). It seems clear, in any case, that Kyd emerged with a solid knowledge of Latin literature and fluency in French and Italian-as manifest in later compositions and translations attributed to him.

Very little is known about Kyd's life in his early twenties. Evidence suggests that he was involved with the Queen's Company of Players, formed in 1583. By 1587, he seems to have entered the service of an unspecified lord. We know that Kyd's lord patronized a company of players for which Christopher Marlowe (1564-1593) also most likely wrote. Furthermore, Kyd dedicated his translation of the French *Cornelia* to the Countesse of Sussex, suggesting his tie to that specific house. The most likely candidate for Kyd's patron, then, emerges as the fourth Earl of Sussex, Henry Radcliffe, with the alternate possibility of the Lord Strange.

The best-documented events of Kyd's life concern his dealings with Christopher Marlowe. In early May 1593, Kyd was arrested by the Queen's Privy Council for possession of heretical and blasphemous papers. On 12 May 1593 he was certainly in prison, to be interrogated thoroughly about the origins of his papers. Kyd confessed that he had received the papers from Marlowe. He later wrote to Sir John Puckering of the Privy Council, disclaiming any intimate relationship with the heretical playwright. But more than anything else-as Freeman duly points out-the humble tone of the letter bears witness to the brutal treatment Kyd received in prison (28). As such, the accuracy of its portrait of Kyd's relationship to Marlowe remains questionable. Marlowe, in any case, had already died of a stabbing wound through the eye on 30 May of the same year.

Kyd himself did not live very long after Marlowe's gruesome demise. The local parish register records his burial on 15 August 1594. His parents chose not to administer his estate. Indeed, Thomas Kyd left precious little legacy to the world: apart from *The Spanish Tragedy*, only a small handful of plays and poems (the majority of which were merely initialed by or attributed to him) are left. *The Spanish Tragedy*, however, remains one of the most successful works of the Elizabethan era. Thomas Kyd's name also arises in relation to the *ur-Hamlet*, the alleged lost source of Shakespeare's *Hamlet*, dating from before 1589. In addition, some scholars have even argued that he was the true writer of Shakespearean works such as *King Lear* and *Titus Andronicus*.

About The Spanish Tragedy

The title page of the 1615 edition of Kyd's celebrated play reads:

> The Spanish Tragedie:
> or,
> Hieronimo is mad againe.

In its day, *The Spanish Tragedy* was anonymous. Only in 1773 did the theatrical historian Thomas Hawkins discover, in Thomas Heywood's *Apology for Actors* (1612), the play's assignment to Thomas Kyd. No other external evidence has been able to corroborate this link. Scholars generally agree, however, on the intimate relationship between *The Spanish Tragedy* and Kyd's *Cornelia*, which strongly suggests a common author. Despite the lack of conclusive evidence, very few-if any-scholars have seriously doubted Kyd's authorship of *The Spanish Tragedy*.

The exact date of the play's composition is uncertain. Estimates generally oscillate within the ten-year frame of 1582-1592. Arthur Freeman points out the particular importance of *The Spanish Tragedy*'s date in the study of Elizabethan drama. It is a question of whether the play was the first to stage certain dramatic elements. Freeman writes:

> If the play precedes *The Jew of Malta* and *The Massacre at Paris* it contains the first Machiavellian villain; if it precedes *John a Kent and John a Cumber*, it contains the earliest modern play-within-play; and if it precedes *Titus Andronicus* it may also be styled the first modern revenge tragedy. Given a date before 1587 and *Tamburlaine*, one might incontrovertibly call Kyd's play the first extant modern tragedy, without qualification. (70-1)

Freeman himself proposes tentatively the dates 1585-1587. Based on almost identical evidence, the French scholar Felix Carre puts forth 1587-1588. Another editor, Philip Edwards, prefers to date the play simply at the "upper limit" of the years 1582-1592 (xxvii).

Carre believes that the play, known simply as *Hieronimo* at the time, was the most successful dramatic work of all Elizabethan theater. Not only did myriad authors constantly allude to the play, but between its publication and the reign of Charles I, the work was printed in no less than ten editions-more than twice the number of Shakespeare editions printing during the same time frame. Carre also cites the famous story (recorded in 1631 by Richard Brathwaite) of a dying woman who exclaimed on her deathbed: "Hieronimo, Hieronimo, O let me see Hieronimo acted!" (41). Whether *The Spanish Tragedy* was *the* single most successful play or not, its immense popularity remains indisputable.

Much of the play's popularity undoubtedly derives from its modernity, or simply, its innovative qualities. Kyd employs dramaturgical devices that are subtle, varied, and at times shocking-the most memorable including the play-within-play and the on-stage revelation of Horatio's body. Kyd's use of language serves as an appropriate counterpart to such imaginative theatricality. One might characterize his style as generally well-balanced. As opposed to Marlowe's sensational prose or Shakespeare's rich verbal foliage, Kyd's language is at times delicate, at times direct; as Freeman notes, he refrains from overtaxing images and metaphors (81). Kyd's language, then, seems particularly well-suited to a play so packed with vivid action.

Apropos of the language, the play's frequent Latin phrases may strike the contemporary reader as unusual. In an extended analysis of *The Spanish Tragedy*, Peter Murray observes that Kyd borrows a significant amount of material from the Roman philosopher and poet Seneca (circa 4 B.C.E.-65 C.E.). The play's opening is modeled on Seneca's *Thyestes*, for example, and many phrases are citations or adaptations of Senecan lines (12). This sort of borrowing was common practice among playwrights at the time. For weaving in a good amount of material in Latin, however, Kyd has been called pretentious and has sometimes been ridiculed. A common audience certainly would have been lost by Hieronimo's fourteen-line monologue at the end of Act 2, though Freeman suggests that "it is a mistake to suppose that even an unlettered audience would be altogether alienated by a few appropriate reflections in so familiar a second language" (83). All phrases in Latin and other foreign languages, in any case, are translated with annotations in the section "Marginalia of The Spanish Tragedy" of this ClassicNote.

Character List

Ghost of Andrea

A Spanish nobleman, Don Andrea has been recently killed in battle by the Portuguese prince Balthazar. His Ghost has now returned from the underworld to witness his former lover Bellimperia kill Balthazar.

Revenge

Sent by the Queen of Hades, Proserpine, Revenge leads the Ghost of Andrea back from the underworld to witness (and create) havoc on earth.

King of Spain

Brother to the Duke of Castile. The King desires a marriage between Balthazar and Bellimperia, the Duke's daughter. He plays a relatively passive role in the play, serving as a good and just monarch-albeit one sometimes lacking in acumen.

Cyprian Duke of Castile

Father to Lorenzo and Bellimperia. Like the King, he is a just man within the constraints of a highly patriarchal society (he will force Bellimperia into a politically desirable marriage). His character contrasts with that of Lorenzo.

Lorenzo

The Duke's son. Lorenzo is a man with somewhat mysterious motives, but his duplicitous character reveals itself throughout the play. He manipulates Balthazar and Pedringano in order to orchestrate the death of Horatio. While he clearly finds pleasure in controlling others, his actions are end-based rather than purely driven by villainous desires.

Bellimperia

Lorenzo's sister and Andrea's former lover. She finds "second love" in Horatio, if only partly to spite Balthazar. She eventually stabs Balthazar as a character in Hieronimo's play and commits suicide. Heironimo claims that the suicide is out of love for Andrea, but this point remains a matter of dispute. Her actions in the second half of the play are motivated by the desire to exact revenge.

Viceroy of Portugal

A loving father to Balthazar, the Viceroy is given to rash judgments. He first unjustly condemns Alexandro, then justly - but harshly - dooms Villuppo. As for the marriage between Balthazar and Bellimperia, he gives his wholehearted consent. Having discovered his son to be alive after all, he hopes to relinquish his crown and retire to a solitary life of thanking the heavens in prayer.

Balthazar

The Viceroy's son arrives in Spain as a captive. He is taken by Bellimperia's beauty, which leads him to state that he is in love. With Lorenzo, he roams about freely and contributes to the murder of Horatio. But unlike Lorenzo, Balthazar is a sympathetic - if - naive character.

Hieronimo

The Marshall of Spain, Hieronimo is the highest official to pronounce judgments. The law does not grant justice for his son's murder, however, so he takes the matter into his own hands. It is Hieronimo who stages the play-within-a-play and is ultimately responsible for the deaths of Lorenzo, Balthazar, and the Duke, and arguably Bellimperia. A character given to fits of madness, he is somewhat of a mystery-much like Shakespeare's Hamlet.

Isabella

Hieronimo's wife. Like her husband, Isabella shows signs of madness and eventually commits suicide under deranged conditions (triggered by the murder of Horatio).

Horatio

Son of Hieronimo and Isabella, Horatio returns from the battle with Portugal as captor of Balthazar. Between him and Lorenzo, however, the true captor of Balthazar remains unclear. He was friends with Andrea and becomes Bellimperia's second love. Horatio is murdered under Bellimperia's eyes when the same lady's servant betrays their secret rendezvous to Lorenzo.

Spanish General

The General gives a glorious but grim account of the recent battle to the King and receives a royal chain for his accomplishments. His account of the battle, however, contradicts the later statements of Lorenzo and Horatio-a crucial point in the play's development.

Don Bazulto

An old man who appears along with three citizens to petition Hieronimo for justice. Like, Hieronimo, his son has been murdered.

Portuguese Ambassador

The Ambassador serves as a crucial link between Portugal and Spain. He brings the Viceroy the blissful news of Balthazar's survival. It is also he who brings confirmation of the Balthazar-Bellimperia marriage back to Spain.

Alexandro

A loyal Portuguese nobleman who is unjustly imprisoned through Villuppo's treachery.

Villuppo

A Portuguese nobleman who betrays Alexandro out of desire for reward.

Pedringano

Bellimperia's servant. Blinded by the desire for gold, Pedringano betrays Bellimperia and Horatio. He also murders Balthazar's servant Serberine at Lorenzo's command. The latter plots successfully to have Pedringano sent to the gallows, where the servant finds himself helpless, without the promised royal pardon.

Lorenzo's Page

An incidental character, the page nonetheless serves to show that Lorenzo sends Pedringano an empty box instead of the promised royal pardon.

Don Pedro, the Viceroy's brother; Deputy; Three Citizens; Two Portuguese; Christophil, Bellimperia's custodian; Serberine, Balthazar's servant; Isabella's Maid; Messenger; Hangman; Characters in the two dumb shows; and Company

Minor characters.

Bazardo, a Painter; Pedro and Jacques, Hieronimo's servants

Characters that appear in the anonymous additions to the 1602 edition of the play.

Major Themes

Death Wish

Of the nine deaths that occur on stage (not including Villuppo's and Andrea's), three of them are suicides. Of the three, Isabella and Hieronimo's suicides are the realization of a death wish expressed throughout the play: they desire to join Horatio in death. But this wish is not repeated by the Viceroy, an equally loving father. This difference is intriguing, as Hieronimo and his wife have a reason to delay their deaths (they must exact revenge), whereas nothing holds back the Viceroy-or so it seems. The lack of a real death wish may reflect a politically-oriented part of his character that complicates his desire to live in solitude after he discovers that Balthazar is still alive. Finally, Bellimperia's suicide remains an unexplained aspect of the play. Why does she unnecessarily keep to her role in Hieronimo's play-within-a-play? Hieronimo's explanation that she loved Andrea too much is unsatisfactory at best. Her death thus shows a vague but strong link between the fulfillment of revenge and the death wish.

Revenge

The Spanish Tragedy is a revenge tragedy. Its very premise is put forth by the character from the underworld named Revenge. But what exactly *is* revenge? A principle, an act, a desire for satisfaction, or something else altogether? The premise of the play may suggest that revenge is indeed an arbitrary matter. Andrea, after all, was slain *in battle* by Balthazar, and this does not seem reason enough for the large-scale revenge tragedy that follows. In any case, Hieronimo, Bellamira-and to an extent Balthazar-all act out of the desire for revenge. The play-within-a-play in the fourth act marks the culmination of this desire. The acting of revenge resolves all the tensions of the play in one blow. Incidentally, the term "avenge" did not carry the modern-day connotation of the act of inflicting punishment as retributive justice; like the connotation of "revenge" today, it also pointed to the infliction of pain in retaliation for a real or imaginary wrong.

Betrayal

Betrayal is an important force in the play. Villuppo's betrayal of Alexandro parallels Lorenzo's betrayal of Horatio-which ostensibly gives birth to the revenge tragedy. Revenge and betrayal therefore go hand in hand. But as opposed to revenge, betrayal can be questioned for its motives. In some cases the motives are clear: Villuppo betrays his fellow nobleman for gold and royal preference; Lorenzo betrays Serberine and Pedringano in order to silence them forever; Bellimperia betrays her brother and Balthazar for love and revenge. It is not so clear, however, why Lorenzo lures Balthazar into betraying Horatio (it would make more sense if Balthazar were the one who plotted the murder). Even more mysterious is Hieronimo's killing of the Duke-an act that betrays his country and must be called murder. Perhaps this final action must be understood in light of Hieronimo's silence, as the Duke attempts to make him betray the cryptic "thing which [he has] vowed inviolate." The play is testament, in any case, to the ubiquity of betrayal in places burdened by power and wealth.

Justice/Injustice

Much of the play centers around questions of justice and injustice. The King must justly divide the reward for Balthazar's capture; the Viceroy punishes Alexandro for injustice (which is itself later revealed to be unjust); Hieronimo is called upon to grant justice as the Marshall of Spain, but the King does not serve justice when it comes to Horatio's murder. Through all of the above-as well as other instances-the play returns to the ancient question of justice. Perhaps most famously in *The Republic*, Socrates discusses its elusive nature: what exactly is justice? Although Hieronimo believes that it can be found in heaven, justice is inextricably linked to revenge in the play-and revenge comes from the underworld. As such, it remains an obscure principle.

Love and Hate

One of Revenge's claims is that he will turn "love to mortal hate." The two resemble the two faces of a coin: one is present where the other is absent. Andrea's love for Bellimperia, for example, instills in Bellimperia a hate for Balthazar. This in turn motivates her to find "second love" in Andrea's friend Horatio, as the young man will further her hate. But this second love itself soon transforms into hate, as Lorenzo and Balthazar murder Horatio. In a similar fashion, the various expressions of love in hate in the play can all be linked together. It is curious that two emotions so diametrically opposed should be found in such proximity. One must undergo a violent transformation to move from love to hate, and perhaps such movements give birth to the powerful drives called madness and revenge.

Madness

In anticipation of Shakespeare's *Hamlet*, Hieronimo and Isabella both become mad after Horatio is murdered - Hieronimo in an active, rampant manner, and Isabella in a passive, oppressed way. Hieronimo's case is particularly interesting, as his madness both propels and delays the tragedy. His paroxysms manifest in soliloquies, and his strange visions build tension, at the same time effectively pushing back the final act of revenge. The sickness therefore serves both as a psychological effect and as a dramatic device. In a similar vein, Hieronimo seems to sometimes forget his purpose over the course of the long third act - only to be reminded by the words "Horatio" or "murder." Is it possible for a memory so strong to be periodically suppressed? Perhaps the memory must protect itself against the death wish so clearly manifest in Hieronimo's dagger and halter.

Theatricality and Obscurity

Two dumb shows occur in the play: the first, one that Hieronimo stages for the King, and the second, one that Revenge stages for the Ghost. Dumb shows, at least in *The Spanish Tragedy*, are marked by their relative obscurity. They must be explained verbally to be understood. In this sense, both Hieronimo's frantic act of digging in Act 3 Scene and the play-within-a-play that he stages in Act 4 Scene 4 are like dumb shows. Accompanied by disjointed or foreign dialogue, they cannot be comprehended without further explanation. What is the purpose, then, of staging such shows? The first masque, at least, has entertainment value. The second could have just as easily been put into words by Revenge. In the third Hieronimo undermines his appeal to the King. And the play-within-a-play, though ostensibly logical in the plot, remains a decidedly strange way to exact revenge. However, it is precisely because of their strangeness and ambiguity that the four shows are central to the tragedy. They show that many events can be baffling - and so can words, as the royal audience's incomprehension of Hieronimo in the last act shows. Reality, perhaps, is not merely *represented* but *presented* on stage: it is something incomprehensible to the players, yet sensible from the vantage point of the chorus.

Glossary of Terms

Behoove

To be necessary; to require; to oblige.

Bower

An arbor or a rustic cottage.

Censure

Opinion or assessment, without negative connotations, as in "the King's censure."

Close with

To meet secretly with.

Coy it

To affect shyness, as in "Although she coy it, as becomes her kind" (II.iii.3).

Despite

Hatred.

Doom

A decision or judgment, without negative connotations. A phrase like "Will both abide the censure of my doom," for example, can address a positive issue (I.ii.175).

Entreat

To beg; to ask earnestly.

Fortune

A neutral word, as Fortune's Wheel brings a subject both high and low.

Gallery

An upper stage from where important guests can watch a play on the main stage.

Gear

Affairs or business, as in "When shall we to this gear?" (III.vi.23)

Guerdon

A reward.

Infect

As an adjective, the word indicates something that is infected and thus tainted or poisonous.

Miracle

A supernatural event; a wonder in the most neutral sense of the word, as in "What means this unexpected miracle?" (III.ii.32)

Pompous

Characterized by splendor and magnificence (in this context, without disparaging connotations).

Scutcheon

Usually spelled "escutcheon"; a shield with a coat of arms depicted.

Sound

To measure the depths of something; figuratively, to understand or comprehend, as in "I sound not well the mystery" (I.v.24).

Train

A body of attendants, such as the king's retinue.

Valiancy

A variant of valiance; bravery, valor, courage.

Wrought

An archaic form of "worked."

Short Summary

In the introduction to the play, the Ghost of the Spanish courtier Don Andrea explains its history. After Andrea was slain in a battle against Portugal, his Ghost made its way through the underworld, only to find itself sent back to earth. The character Revenge, his guide, tells him that he has been sent back to witness his former lover Bellimperia kill Balthazar, the "author of [his] death." The Ghost and Revenge sit down to watch the spectacle unfold.

In the opening act, the Spanish forces return from their victory over Portugal. The General gives an account of the battle to the King, explaining that they have reached a state of "peace conditional" and that they have captured the Portuguese prince Balthazar. The Duke of Castile's son Lorenzo and the Marshall Hieronimo's son Horatio, however, dispute their respective roles in capturing the Portuguese prince. The King rewards them both. Meanwhile, in Portugal, the Viceroy laments his son's death. The loyal Alexandro tells him that his son is in fact still alive. Another nobleman, Villuppo, however, declares that he saw Alexandro shoot Balthazar in the back. Alexandro is immediately imprisoned.

In Spain, Horatio recounts the battle to Bellimperia, Lorenzo's sister and Andrea's former lover. The two begin to fall in love. In the same scene, Balthazar also expresses his love for Bellimperia. The Portuguese ambassador arrives, and Hieronimo stages a masque for him and the King. The act closes with Revenge foreboding a general demise.

In the second act, the King of Spain attempts to arrange a marriage between Bellimperia and Balthazar. Bellimperia, however, is in love with Horatio. As the two make their way to a secluded bower, the servant Pedringano betrays them to Lorenzo and Balthazar. Horatio is hung from an arbor and stabbed to death. Hieronimo enters to find his son's body and vows revenge. The Ghost expresses dismay at the turn of events, but Revenge advises him to be patient.

The Viceroy discovers the truth about his son in the third act. He immediately sets Alexandro free and condemns Villuppo to a painful death. In Spain, Bellimperia is held captive, but manages to send Hieronimo a letter in which she reveals the identity of Horatio's killers. Lorenzo, on the other hand, attempts to purge all evidence of the murder. He makes Pedringano shoot Serberine (Balthazar's servant who was present at the murder scene), and then plots successfully to have Pedringano himself hanged. Pedringano's last (undelivered) letter to Lorenzo, however, falls into Hieronimo's hands. Hieronimo thus confirms Bellimperia's accusations and resolves to demand justice before the King. At home, his wife Isabelle "runs lunatic."

Like his wife, Hieronimo shows distinct signs of madness. He contemplates suicide, but again vows to first exact revenge for Horatio's death. The Portuguese ambassador, meanwhile, arrives with good news: the Viceroy has consented to the marriage between Balthazar and Bellimperia (whom Lorenzo has just released from captivity). Hieronimo calls for justice before the King, but undermines himself by falling into a frenzy. Later, several citizens come to petition Hieronimo, but once again Hieronimo is carried away in an ecstatic fit.

The Viceroy himself arrives at the end of the act. While the nuptial celebrations are prepared, the Duke confronts Lorenzo and Hieronimo about the negative rumors surrounding the two. Hieronimo denies any wrongdoing on Lorenzo's part, and Bellimperia seems to have reconciled with Balthazar. The Ghost is alarmed at such an unexpected turn of events, but Revenge once again reassures him that all is well (or, for the characters in the tragedy, quite amiss).

In the final act, Bellimperia and Hieronimo work together to exact their revenge on Lorenzo and Balthazar. Hieronimo wrote a tragedy in his youth, which the two young men now act out for the royal audience. Back in the arbor where Horatio was murdered, Isabella commits suicide. As for Hieronimo's play, the plot is executed smoothly, and Lorenzo and Balthazar are killed on stage. Bellimperia, too, commits suicide. The King, the Viceroy, and the Duke are all horrified when they discover that the play seemed to merely be a simulation. They demand to know Hieronimo's motives, but the latter bites off his tongue, stabs the Duke, and finally commits suicide.

Summary and Analysis of Act 1

Act 1, Scene 1

The Ghost of Andrea enters the scene to deliver a monologue and put forth the premises of the play. When he was alive, the Ghost states, he served as a courtier in the Spanish court. In the prime of his youth he engaged in a secret love affair with the Duke of Castile's daughter, Bellimperia. Spain's war with Portugal, however, ended his blissful days and separated him from his love. The Ghost recounts how Don Andrea was slain in battle and his soul descended to the gates of the underworld, where it had to wait three days for the Marshall's son Horatio to perform the rites of burial.

Andrea's body properly buried, his soul made its way past Cerberus (the three-headed dog guarding the gate to Hades), only to find itself in front of the three judges of the underworld: Minos, Aeacus and Rhadamanth. Minos declared that Don Andrea lived and died in love, prompting Aeacus to vote to send him to the "fields of love." Rhadamanth dissented, however, claiming that Don Andrea died in war and should thus go to the "martial fields" instead. Minos finally deferred judgment to Pluto, lord of the underworld. The soul of Andrea proceeded through the underworld, passing by many horrifying sights before arriving at Pluto's tower in the middle of a fair Elysian field. He encountered Pluto, but it was the queen of Hades Proserpine who passed his final judgment.

As it turns out, the Ghost was addressing the character Revenge as much as the audience. Once the Queen bade Revenge to lead Don Andrea's soul through the gates of horn, he found himself in his current place. Rather than an explanation for the turn of events, Revenge responds with a promise: the Ghost will see Balthazar - who took Andrea's life - killed by Bellimperia. The two then sit down as spectators to a play. Revenge states: "Here sit we down to see the mystery, / And serve for Chorus in this tragedy."

Act 1, Scene 2

The King of Spain enters with his brother the Duke of Castile, the Marshall Hieronimo, and a General. The King asks for a battle report, and the General declares that Spain achieved victory with little loss to itself. Portugal will honor Spain and its tribute. The King then requests a more detailed account of the military success and the General gladly obliges. After painting a picture of the battlefield in its poetic glory as well as its grim details, the General says that Don Andrea and his men fought so bravely as to push the Portuguese soldiers into retreat. The Portuguese prince, Balthazar, challenged Andrea and killed him, but Hieronimo's son Horatio, in turn, defeated Balthazar and took him prisoner, effectively assuring the Spanish victory.

After hearing the good news reconfirmed, the King rewards the General with a chain. The latter states that a "peace conditional" has been reached with Portugal, whereby the Spanish forces will keep their peace so long as Portugal pays its tribute. The King then turns to Hieronimo and promises him and his son a reward. At this point a trumpet sounds, and the army files through the King's hall. Balthazar marches between Horatio and the Duke's son Lorenzo. The King calls for Balthazar to be brought before him and dismisses everyone else, granting every soldier two ducats and every leader ten as a reward.

The Portuguese prince presents himself meekly before the Spanish King, who receives him magnanimously: Balthazar shall be kept in Spain, well and alive, though not at liberty per se. At this point the King asks whether it is Horatio or Lorenzo who holds Balthazar prisoner. The two argue over the privilege, each vaunting his own accomplishment in capturing the prince. While Balthazar submits himself to both of the young men, Hieronimo speaks in his son's favor. The King finally pronounces his decision: Lorenzo will hold Balthazar captive and receive his weapons and horse; Horatio will receive the prince's armor, as well as his ransom. Before retiring, the King encourages Horatio to visit Balthazar, as the prince seems to think very fondly of him.

Act 1, Scene 3

The scene shifts to Portugal, where the Viceroy laments his misfortune in front of two noblemen, Alexandro and Villuppo. After confirming that an ambassador has been sent to Spain with the required tribute, the Viceroy prostrates himself on the ground. This way, he declares, his fortunes can no fall no further. The Viceroy continues to grieve over his misfortunes and in particular over the loss of his son - if only he himself could have been killed, instead of Balthazar! Alexandro hastens to inform the King that his son is most likely still alive: the prince has been taken prisoner, and his ransom will probably assure his life.

Villuppo, however, tells a different tale. After insuring against the King's wrath for being the messenger of bad news, Villuppo claims that he saw Balthazar engaged in battle with the Spanish General, whereupon Alexandro shot the prince in the back. Despite Alexandro's vehement protest, the Viceroy is inclined to believe Villuppo. His nightly dreams, the Viceroy says, have confirmed Villuppo's claim that the Spanish dragged Balthazar's body to their tents.

The Viceroy thus turns to Alexandro and accuses him of treachery, speculating that he was blinded by either the Spanish gold or his eventual claim to the throne. The Viceroy takes his crown off and puts it on again, declaring that he will wear it until Alexandro's blood has been spilled. He sends Alexandro to prison and promises Villuppo a reward. The latter delivers a short soliloquy to conclude the scene, revealing desire for a reward as his motive for treachery.

Act 1, Scene 4

Back in Spain, Bellimperia entreats Horatio to explain to her the circumstances of Don Andrea's death. Horatio states that Andrea was engaged with Balthazar in a fierce duel when the goddess Nemesis, envious of Andrea's "praise and worth," came to Balthazar's aid. The Portuguese prince, thus at an unfair advantage, was able to kill Andrea before Horatio could come to his rescue. Horatio then explains that he honored the corpse with a proper funeral, only taking a scarf as a keepsake. Bellimperia, whose last gift to her lover was the very same scarf, promises Horatio her gratitude and friendship. Horatio in turn promises to serve the lady and leaves to look for Balthazar. Alone on stage, Bellimperia admits her "second love" for Horatio and resolves to seek out proper vengeance on the Portuguese prince.

Lorenzo and Balthazar enter to find Bellimperia all alone in a melancholic mood. In a series of short exchanges, Balthazar professes his love for the fair Bellimperia. Just as Bellimperia drops her glove, however, Horatio enters the scene to pick it up for her. Lorenzo promises to dispel his sister's cloudy mood, and the three men head to the feast welcoming the Portuguese ambassador.

Act 1, Sccnc 5

The King of Spain welcomes the Portuguese ambassador. The ambassador is glad to see that Balthazar is alive and well, contrary to his expectations. All sit down to the banquet, whereupon Hieronimo enters to stage a masque.

Three knights enter the stage and take three kings captive by removing their crowns. Hieronimo takes the first knight's escutcheon ("scutcheon") and gives it to the first king; according to Hieronimo's narration, the knight plays the Earl of Gloucester, who once conquered Portugal and made it bear the English monarchy's coat of arms. The same performance takes place for the second knight and king, between England and Portugal, respectively. The third pair, however, represents the Duke of Lancaster conquering the King of Spain.

History shows, therefore, that neither party need be insulted by the outcome of the recent battle. After the masque, the King praises Hieronimo for pleasing both the Portuguese ambassador and himself.

Act 1, Scene 6

Finding nothing pleasant in the sight of Balthazar feasting merrily, the Ghost of Andrea asks Revenge why they have been watching the above events unfold. As a response, Revenge concludes the act with an ominous presage:

> I'll turn their friendship into fell despite,
> Their love to mortal hate, their day to night,
> Their hope into despair, their peace to war,
> Their joys to pain, their bliss to misery. (I.i.6-9)

Analysis

F. S. Boas believes that "few passages in Elizabethan literature were so often quoted and caricatured" as the opening lines of The Spanish Tragedy (393):

> When this eternal substance of my soul
> Did live imprison'd in my wanton flesh,
> Each in their function serving other's need,
> I was a courtier in the Spanish court:
> My name was Don Andrea. (I.i.1-5)

"Caricatured" is a misleading word. As Arthur Freeman suggests, the parodies may be akin to the innumerable burlesques on Hamlet's famous "To be or not to be" (81). The corollary of such a parallel is that Kyd's opening lines may reflect a profound truth about human existence. In the world of the play, at least, the soul and the flesh exist as separate entities, each dependant on the other. Though the soul may be eternal, it cannot escape the prison of the flesh. The two exist therefore in a sort of mutualism, but one in which conflicts certainly arise: the passions of the "wanton flesh" may at times lead the soul in undesirable directions.

The descent into the underworld narrated by the Ghost of Andrea recalls that of Aeneas's descent in Book VI of Virgil's *Aeneid*. It is noteworthy, however, that Revenge takes the Ghost through the gates of horn. The gates refer to the following famous passage in the *Aeneid*:

> There are two gates of Sleep, one said to be
> Of horn, whereby the true shades pass with ease,
> The other all white ivory agleam
> Without a flaw, and yet false dreams are sent
> Through this one by the ghosts to the upper world. (vi. 1211-1215)

Aeneas passes through the ivory gates of "false dreams." What does it mean, then, for the Ghost to have come through the gates of horn?

The question seems to be intimately bound up with the "theatricality" of the main play. In other words, the Ghost and Revenge sit down to watch a play that unfolds before their eyes. While the exposition progresses from the second to the fifth scene, they are spectators invisible to the characters as well as to the audience. But as spectators, they also walk on the same stage as the characters in the first and last scene of the act. To complicate matters further, Revenge indicates that he has foresight as well as control over the events of the play. All of this is suggestive of a parallel between the actual audience and the two spectators. The audience, after all, could potentially fulfill the roles of Ghost and Revenge - as actors, a playwright, or simply one who knows how the play will end. The gates of horn, then, may attest to the proximity of the play to reality - at least in a symbolic sense.

It is not clear, however, whether an objective "reality" can exist even in the world of The Spanish Tragedy. The events surrounding Balthazar in the battle, for example, are hopelessly confused in the opening act. The Lord General tells a poetic but vague story of a "single fight" between Horatio and Balthazar; both Horatio and Lorenzo each tell a version that contradicts the General's version, and in Portugal Villuppo invents an entirely different version altogether. When recounting the turn of events to Bellimperia, furthermore, Horatio claims that the goddess Nemesis granted divine aid to Balthazar in defeating Andrea. Perhaps it makes the most sense to first follow the General's version, and then to assume that Lorenzo and Horatio both fought Balthazar. But it may also be a mistake to believe that everything should make sense.

In a play that's premise is a seemingly whimsical decision passed by the Queen of Hades, the plot may not necessarily follow a clear linear progression. The existence of a "higher" (inaccessible) order finds a loose parallel in Hieronimo's masque. The Marshall pleases both his king and the Portuguese ambassador by showing that both of their countries have been previously conquered by English forces (the history told is only partly accurate, but surely would have pleased an English audience). History, in a large sense, is composed of small stories. With such a perspective, neither Spain nor Portugal should worry about the recent battle. But this larger history usually remains inaccessible; the King "sound[s] not well the mystery" until Hieronimo explains the significance of the masque. Plays-within-plays, most of them simply dumb shows, will be important throughout the play.

In light of the above, the world of The Spanish Tragedy becomes unstable and volatile. The King, who so spontaneously rewards the General with a chain, does not quite know how to deal with Horatio and Lorenzo. Before issuing an awkward partition of their reward for capturing Balthazar, he must first reaffirm his authority: "Will both abide the censure of my doom"? Across the border, the Portuguese Viceroy finds himself on even more unstable sands. The evidence that inspires him to believe Villuppo's story instead of Alexandro's is nothing but his oneiric visions. And his dreams, as the audience perceives, are simply false. Moreover, his interpretation of the vision as confirming Villuppo's accusation remains entirely whimsical. Or perhaps not only does "evil news fly faster still than good"; it also flies with more credibility. In any case, the Viceroy undermines his own authority in the opening act of the play. This is symbolically reflected in his removal of the crown - which he immediately puts back on. The sovereign who abdicates his own power, if such a thing is possible, should not have the authority to take back the same sovereignty.

The exposition, then, has set up an explosive potential for murder, hate, and revenge, coupled with love. With Bellimperia, love and revenge will merge together in a sub-plot surrounding Horatio. The action of the play, however, has just only begun. As the Ghost duly notes, the promised death of Balthazar is still nowhere in sight. But Revenge promises much more than his initial statement - indeed, a massively chaotic event that will turn the order of things upside down.

Summary and Analysis of Act 2

Act 2, Scene 1

Lorenzo tries to comfort Balthazar with regards to Bellimperia, suggesting that in due time she will come to like the Portuguese prince. Balthazar expresses his unconsoled spirit in a short pessimistic monologue. Lorenzo assures him that they will find out the reason behind Bellimperia's coldness; he has already formulated a plan to uncover the truth.

Lorenzo calls Bellimperia's servant Pedringano to the scene. Lorenzo speaks of a past favor that he granted Pedringano: when the Duke of Castile discovered Pedringano's role as a go-between for Andrea and Bellimperia, Lorenzo protected the servant from the Duke's wrath. The same prince now promises Pedringano an additional favor of a gold chain - should he simply speak the truth. Pedringano agrees, and Lorenzo asks him about the nature of Bellimperia's love since Andrea's death. Who loves her, and who does she love? The servant claims ignorance, but Lorenzo draws his sword in response and threatens to kill him. Pedringano finally admits that Bellimperia loves Horatio. He has perused the love letters that she sent Horatio. Lorenzo grants him the reward and, promising a further reward, demands to be notified when the "lovers meet." Balthazar thus resolves to take revenge on Horatio, despite the risks involved:

> Thus hath he ta'en my body by his force,
> And now by sleight would captivate my soul:
> But in his fall I'll tempt the destinies,
> And either lose my life, or win my love. (II.i.130-133)

Act 2, Scene 2

essay.

Horatio and Bellimperia enter the scene. Pedringano, pointing out the lovers for Lorenzo and Balthazar, places the two princes in hiding. Horatio wonders why, their love now made so clear, Bellimperia shows signs of "inward languishments." Bellimperia responds through an extended metaphor, comparing her heart to a sailing ship: she is still recovering from stormy times (presumably Andrea's death), and now seeks refuge in the port that is Horatio's love. Hidden above, Balthazar expresses his dismay, but Lorenzo looks on gleefully - for he already envisions "Horatio's fall." The two lovers continue their dialogue and soon agree to meet in a secluded field the very same evening. In the meantime, however, they must hide their love from the Duke of Castile. Lorenzo concludes the scene with a promise to send "[Horatio's] soul into eternal night."

Act 2, Scene 3

The King of Spain enters with the Duke of Castile and the Portuguese ambassador.

The King asks the Duke what Bellimperia thinks of Balthazar. The Duke responds that while his daughter disclaims any love for the Portuguese prince at the moment, she will in time heed his advice - "Which is to love him, or forgo [her father's] love." The King thus asks the ambassador to advise the Viceroy in favor of a marriage between Bellimperia and Balthazar. The advantages for Portugal will be many: it will receive a generous dowry, its tribute will be released, and it will be intimately linked to the Spanish crown. The King finally requests that the Viceroy set the marriage date and reminds the ambassador to bring Balthazar's ransom for Horatio. After the ambassador leaves, the King once again turns to the Duke of Castile and presses him to convince Bellimperia in favor of the marriage - for the good of Spain.

Act 2, Scene 4

Horatio and Bellimperia meet in the field and walk towards a bower. To guard against anyone approaching, Bellimperia entrusts Pedringano to guard the gate, but he reveals his treacherous intentions in an aside. The two lovers engage in amorous talk, but just as their intimacy increases, Lorenzo and Balthazar enter the scene with Serberine and Pedringano (the latter in disguise). The men take Bellimperia aside, hang up Horatio, and then stab him. Bellimperia pleads for Horatio's life and then manages to cry for help before the men take her and leave the scene of murder.

Act 2, Scene 5

Hieronimo enters in his nightshirt, having been awaked by a woman's cry for help. To his dismay, he finds a hanged man - and suspects that the murderers have attempted to incriminate him. Upon cutting the corpse down, however, he recognizes it as his son Horatio. Hieronimo breaks down into a tormented soliloquy, apostrophizing his dead son. His wife Isabella enters the scene and commiserates with him, whereupon Hieronimo vows to exact due revenge: his son's bloody handkerchief will not leave him until he kills the murderers - and neither will the corpse be buried! The two carry off the corpse, and Hieronimo concludes the scene with a monologue in Latin (see section "Marginalia in The Spanish Tragedy" of this ClassicNote for a translation and brief commentary).

Act 2, Scene 6

The Ghost once again questions Revenge's motives. Why has he been made to witness men kill his friend Horatio and abuse his love Bellimperia? Revenge advises him to remain patient, reaffirming Balthazar's imminent downfall.

Analysis

From the opening of the second act, Lorenzo shows himself to be a scheming villain. A man of his position wields a significant amount of power: he can easily afford to both bribe and threaten Pedringano, and thus obtain information about Bellimperia's most private secret. But what could be Lorenzo's motive in helping Balthazar? The most sympathetic reading would suggest that he disapproves of his sister's private affair with Horatio. Any loyal brother would be outraged to find his sister in a secluded field, clearly engaged in an illicit relationship, yet the unpleasant episode with Pedringano demonstrates that Lorenzo can make no such claim to righteousness, or, for that matter, brotherly feelings. Besides, the Spanish prince attests his loyalty to Balthazar from the very opening lines of the scene, and the audience has no reason to believe that he is lying. So perhaps it is simply a matter of rivalry and jealousy. In the previous act, after all, even the sovereign King hesitated between Lorenzo and Horatio's respective claims to glory.

Whatever his motives, Lorenzo serves as a lens through which Balthazar and Pedringano pass to focus on Horatio's death. Love becomes hate: Lorenzo's love for Balthazar, Balthazar's love for Bellimperia, and Pedringano's love for gold are all channeled into Balthazar's desire for revenge. The Portuguese prince may, incidentally, be the least culpable of the three conspirators. In contrast with Lorenzo's vileness, Balthazar's earnest monologue at the end of the first scene speaks to his genuine and sincere character. He has indeed found both his body and soul captured by Horatio, so a desire for personal revenge may only be natural - just as natural, in any case, as Bellimperia's desire to take revenge on Balthazar. In both cases love has been transformed into hate.

The resulting murder of Horatio is criminal and cruel. The murder scene undoubtedly marks the climax of the sub-plot surrounding Horatio, and it consequently sets Hieronimo's quest for revenge in motion. Quartos published in and after 1615 feature a woodcut of the murder scene with Horatio hanging in a tree. In all its appearances of injustice, however, it is not clear whether the law would condemn the murder very harshly. Horatio and Bellimperia are, after all, carrying out their affair in hiding from the law (the Duke and the King). To illustrate the point with an extreme example: where does justice stand when a murder kills another murderer? Later in the play, Hieronimo will be forced to negotiate between juridical and personal justice.

Meanwhile, the consequences of the murder are upheld by the King of Spain in a twist of dramatic irony. Bellimperia will be forced to marry none other than Balthazar, whether she likes it or not. Conversely, the preceding murder scene becomes even more excessive and pointless. The arranged marriage will return to Balthazar both his soul (Bellimperia) and his body (he will rise to rule over Horatio through his heir). The Portuguese prince thus retrospectively loses his motives for revenge. Behind all such confusion, Revenge's massive scheme begins to show its destructive contours.

Even as the plot takes quick dramatic turns, the staging details should not be overlooked. Objects take on particular significance as things thrown against the mind (etymologically *ob* + *jectum* = "thrown against"). To both Balthazar and Horatio, Bellimperia's dropped glove in the first act becomes an extension of her hand, and thus a metonym for her favor. Similarly in the second act, Horatio's handkerchief becomes in Hieronimo's mind a projection of his son's presence, or a metonymy for the unburied corpse. Full of blood and sweat, it is as if Horatio continues to circulate in the play - and he indeed does, as the audience will later see.

Through the emphasis on select objects, Kyd evokes the poetics of stage-space. The audience notices that Lorenzo and Balthazar hide *above* in the second scene of the act. From the heights, the two men both envision Horatio's "fall." When they actually murder Horatio, however, they hang him *up*; it is Hieronimo who actually takes the body down. In a literal sense, then, neither Lorenzo nor Balthazar have yet to see "Horatio's fall." This will come later in the play, with dire consequences. In the meantime, the attention to space and height will be taken up again when the curtains are lifted for the third act.

Summary and Analysis of Act 3, Scenes 1-10

Act 3, Scene 1

In Portugal, the Viceroy laments his fate - thrown from the heights of glory to the depths of despair, and by hate deprived of a son! A nobleman remarks that he never would have suspected hate in Alexandro's heart. The "countenance" of words, it seems, cannot be trusted. Villuppo continues to incriminate Alexandro but the Viceroy cuts him off in anger - the traitor shall be summoned and condemned to death.

Alexandro enters with a nobleman who encourages him to "hope the best." In front of the Viceroy, Alexandro insists on his innocence in vain. His body is bound to a stake, and preparations are made to burn him alive. Now turning to Villuppo, Alexandro declares that his "guiltless death will be aveng'd." At this point the Ambassador arrives with news from Spain: Balthazar is alive and well. The Viceroy, reading through the letters from Spain, immediately sets Alexandro free and demands to know Villuppo's motives for betrayal. The latter submits himself humbly to the Viceroy, expressing remorse for his shameless desire "for reward and hope to be preferr'd." The Viceroy sends Villuppo away, brushing aside Alexandro's movement to entreat for mercy. All exit to settle matters with Spain and commemorate Alexandro's loyalty.

Act 3, Scene 2

Hieronimo enters the scene, still bemoaning his son's death in a series of apostrophes. He cries to the heavens for justice in form of revenge and continues his monologue until a letter suddenly falls from the sky. The letter is from Bellimperia - written in blood for want of ink - and informs Hieronimo that Balthazar and Lorenzo conspired together the kill his son. Hieronimo suspects a trap, and thus warily sets out to confirm Bellimperia's accusations.

Pedringano enters, followed by Lorenzo. The prince explains that Bellimperia has been confined by the Duke for "some disgrace." He offers to hear Hieronimo's request in place of Bellimperia, but Hieronimo declines and leaves the scene. Suspecting Serberine of revealing the truth about Horatio's murder, Lorenzo gives Pedringano gold and sends him to kill Serberine the very same night. Lorenzo then reveals his dual manipulation: he will send guards on patrol to capture Pedringano in the act of murdering Serberine, thus ridding himself of future risks. As he puts it: "better it's that base companions die, / Than by their life to hazard our good haps."

Act 3, Scene 3

Pedringano enters with a pistol in his hand. He expresses his qualms about the prospect of shooting Serberine but is comforted by the thought of his reward. Also reassuring is the belief that, should he be captured, Lorenzo will protect him. Three guards arrive in the meantime, wondering why they have been commanded to watch such a secluded place. Serberine comes on scene, and Pedringano shoots him almost immediately. The guards in turn capture Pedringano and take him to see Hieronimo.

Act 3, Scene 4

The following morning, Lorenzo confesses his fears to Balthazar: he believes that their crime has been betrayed to Hieronimo. A page enters to announce that Serberine has been killed by Pedringano. Balthazar is outraged, and Lorenzo advises him to take due vengeance by complaining to the King of Spain. Balthazar rushes off to see the trials. Alone on stage, Lorenzo gloats over his ability to manipulate the Portuguese prince: "I lay the plot: he prosecutes the point; / I set the trap: he breaks the worthless twigs." A messenger arrives with a request for help from Pedringano, who has been imprisoned. In response Lorenzo sends his page bearing a box and a message: the box contains Lorenzo's signed pardon, which Pedringano shall open only at the very last moment. Alone once again, Lorenzo ponders the course of his fortune. He dares not speak out loud, however, for fear of "unfriendly ears."

Act 3, Scene 5

On the way to find Pedringano in prison, the page is overcome with curiosity and opens the box - only to find nothing inside. He realizes that Lorenzo intends to trick Pedringano. For fear of being hanged himself, however, the page cannot act on his sympathy.

Act 3, Scene 6

Hieronimo remarks on the irony of his profession as Marshall: why should "neither gods nor men be just" to he who judges other men justly? Officers enter with Pedringano, letter in hand, followed by Lorenzo's page. After a series of exchanges, highly impudent on Pedringano's part (he believes the page to carry a royal pardon), Pedringano is taken away by the hangman. Hieronimo expresses outrage over Pedringano's audacity as a convicted murderer, whereupon he suddenly remembers his dead son and exits the scene.

Act 3, Scene 7

Hieronimo is once again alone, deploring the weight of his sufferance. His "tortured soul" has so far has been unable to reach the "empyreal heights" of justice and revenge. The hangman enters frantically with a letter in hand, claiming that they should not have killed Pedringano. Hieronimo sends him away with a promise to protect him from harm and opens the letter: Pedringano has written his final words to Lorenzo, threatening to reveal the truth before he is hanged. From the letter,

Hieronimo deduces that it was Lorenzo and Balthazar who murdered his son. He now realizes the truth behind Bellimperia's letter and resolves to demand justice in front of the King.

Act 3, Scene 8

In Hieronimo's home, Isabella "runs lunatic" despite the maid's best efforts to comfort her. It seems that Horatio's death, combined with the mystery of his murderers, has forced her tormented soul into a frenzy.

Act 3, Scene 9

Bellimperia sits at a window, bemoaning her powerless situation in captivity. She apostrophizes Hieronimo and Andrea before resolving to wait patiently for her release. The custodian Christophil enters to fetch her.

Act 3, Scene 10

Lorenzo enters with Balthazar and confirms Pedringano's death with his page. Deeming the affair to have "o'erblown," Lorenzo decides to set his sister free. He advises Balthazar to "deal cunningly" with Bellimperia just as she arrives, full of fury and contempt. Lorenzo claims that he merely "sought to save [her] honour and [his] own" through his actions; having come to Hieronimo's estate with Balthazar to settle some official matters, he found Bellimperia with Horatio. Upon recalling her "old disgrace" with Andrea and the Duke's consequent wrath, he saw it best to dispose with Horatio and hide his sister away for some time. Bellimperia seems unconvinced, but the dialogue is diverted towards an increasingly cryptic exchange concerning Balthazar, Bellimperia, and their relation to love and fear.

Analysis

The third act opens with the resolution of the sub-plot that takes place in Portugal. The scene may seem superfluous to the larger picture of *The Spanish Tragedy*. Unlike the death of Horatio, the tensions between the Viceroy, Alexandro, and Villuppo bear no direct influence on the outcome of the play. It is precisely because of this ambiguous relation to the rest of the play, however, that the scene raises several important questions.

Like Hieronimo, the Viceroy believes that his son has been unjustly murdered and finds himself in the depths of despair. He would like to lie at the "lowest" point possible so as to avoid falling further (in Act 1 Scene 3, he states in Latin that "He who prostrate hath no where to fall"). But even at such a lifetime low, the Viceroy still sits too high in his throne to commiserate with the equally tormented Alexandro, whose words of protest are suppressed. Luckily, the ambassador soon brings good news from Spain. At this point, the Viceroy is overjoyed and hastily makes amends with Alexandro. Villuppo, in turn, is condemned to the "bitterest torments" - even worse than those prepared for Alexandro. Has justice been served?

This question takes on interesting dimensions when considered in relation to Hieronimo. The Marshall, too, finds himself with a murdered son, and also desires justice. But just as Lorenzo's motive for killing Horatio remains unresolved, so too are their respective claims to having captured Balthazar shrouded in mystery. It is not out of the question that Horatio took undue credit in the battlefield. Men are easily corrupt: the mere desire for gold and glory made Villuppo betray his fellow noblemen. The same can be said for Pedringano, who had presumably been well treated by fair Bellimperia for many years. Thus seen, the Viceroy's initial mistake destabilizes Hieronimo's righteous claim to justice and revenge. Hieronimo may be mistaken to believe Horatio's total innocence in the affair - or, for that matter, Pedringano's damning letter to Lorenzo. Does Hieronimo have a redeeming quality lacking in the Viceroy? All of this will eventually call into question the fine distinction between justice and revenge.

Meanwhile, Lorenzo continues to manipulate friends and foes alike. As a distrustful Machiavellian schemer he anticipates, in many ways, Shakespeare's Iago (the play had its own direct source in Giraldi Cinthio's *Hecatommithi* [1565]). Unlike Iago, however, the Castilian prince is primarily concerned with covering up his tracks. Once the murder is committed, he falls into an almost paranoiac state of mind, whereby both Serberine and Pedringano must be immediately killed off. There is no reason to believe that either of the two would have revealed the truth behind Horatio's murder - especially since they were both present at the crime scene. (Serberine's case is particularly curious, given his entirely undeveloped character; perhaps he serves to show that Lorenzo orchestrates a gratuitous murder.)

Justice or revenge for Hieronimo, then, only emerges out of fear and uncertainty. If Lorenzo had kept Pedringano close to him, Bellimperia's accusations may never have been confirmed. Be betraying Pedringano to the law, Lorenzo involuntarily undoes the order that he has attempted to impose on the stage - a mistake aptly symbolized by the empty box into which the page peeks. The box, in Pedringano trusting eyes, contains the law. It is at once the "righteous" law (a royal pardon) and the law of criminals (mutual trust, without which no criminal organization can operate). By sending a box with nothing but empty promises inside, Lorenzo symbolically obliterates the natural order of things. In other words, he advances the total upheaval that Revenge prophesized at the end of the first act: "I'll turn their friendship into fell despite, / Their love to mortal hate, their day to night," etc.

Also noteworthy in the third act is the introduction of madness into the play. To a certain extent, Revenge's prophesy in the first act already adumbrates madness - if only in a figurative, chaotic sense. In Isabella, however, the word takes on a concrete form. To her maid's alarm, she begins to run around, frantically searching for Horatio *as well as* his killers. While Isabella's scene is short, it suggests an interesting reason, or etiology, behind her madness. Her last words in the scene read: "But say, where shall I find the men, the murderers, / That slew Horatio? Whither shall I run / To find them out that murdered my son?" The impelling force behind her frenzy, it seems, is the frustration of not even knowing the identity of her son's murderers. Her disease is thus the absence of history (recall the discussion of history and stories in the analysis of the first act). And yet she calls for herbs to "purge the heart" - as if the disease were an internal matter, and moreover one of waste. It is this paradoxical intentional/external tension that Hieronimo carries on in the second half of the third act.

Summary and Analysis of Act 3, Scenes 11-15

Act 3, Scene 11

Two Portuguese men enter in search of the Duke of Castile. Hieronimo points out the correct house for them, whereupon it becomes clear that the two men are actually looking for Lorenzo. Hieronimo suddenly embarks on a rant about finding "Despair and Death" on the left-hand path, at the end of which the men will find Lorenzo in a hellish scene. The two men leave the scene, deeming Hieronimo either a "passing lunatic" or one who has lost his wits in old age.

Act 3, Scene 12

Hieronimo enters with dagger and halter in hand. He contemplates committing suicide, but decides against it - after all, "Who would revenge Horatio's murder then?" He throws away the dagger and halter, then picks them up again before the King arrives.

The King and the Portuguese ambassador arrive with the Duke and Lorenzo. Hieronimo cries "Justice, O justice to Hieronimo," but the King does not quite hear him and Lorenzo sends him away. Meanwhile, the ambassador brings good news from Portugal: the Viceroy has consented to the marriage between Balthazar and Bellimperia. He has moreover decided to relinquish the throne to his son, effectively making Bellimperia a queen. As the Spanish King and Duke express their joy, the ambassador mentions that he has also brought Balthazar's ransom.

Upon hearing his son's name, Hieronimo once again cries for the King's attention: "Justice, O, justice, justice, gentle king!" Lorenzo attempts to keep him away, but in vain. Hieronimo exclaims wildly, "Give me my son!" and begins to dig with his dagger, announcing his resignation from the position of Marshall. The King demands for Hieronimo to be restrained, but the latter quickly takes his leave. Lorenzo suggests that Hieronimo has gone mad and that his office should be taken away. The King decides to proceed more prudently, and in the meantime sends Hieronimo the ransom due to his son.

Act 3, Scene 13

Hieronimo enters with a book in hand and delivers a speech that begins "*Vindicta mihi*" ("Revenge is due to me")! Since heaven revenges every ill, Hieronimo declares, he must serve the will of heaven. He has failed to find official redress for his son's murder, and therefore must revenge Horatio's death with his own devices. To do this he will first dissemble quiet and ignorance, thus buying time until he knows "when, where, and how" to take revenge.

A servant brings news of several petitioners who have come to see Hieronimo. Three citizens each voice their complaints and hand in their legal papers. Hieronimo then notices Don Bazulto the senex (Latin for "old man"), who alone stands aside mute. Hieronimo inquires after the senex's suite and in response receives a document titled "*The humble supplication Of Don Bazulto for his murder'd son.*" The title triggers a reaction in Hieronimo: reminded painfully of Horatio's death, he identifies intimately with the old man. Hieronimo takes out his handkerchief for the old man to wipe his eyes, but stops mid-action when he realizes its former owner. Now entirely unsettled, Hieronimo gives the senex his handkerchief as well as his purse.

As if he has forgotten his office as Marshall, Hieronimo delivers an ecstatic monologue about paternal love and the necessity for revenge - even if it entails descending into hell. The rhapsody culminates in Hieronimo tearing the petition papers in an uncanny imitation of tearing apart the limbs of his son's murderers. He leaves the scene, followed by the petitioners, then reappears moments later. One of the petitioners cries that his lease worth ten pounds has been torn up, to which Hieronimo responds that he "gave it never a wound." Indeed caught in a strange rapture, he addresses the senex first as his son, then as a Fury who summons him to the underworld. Hieronimo finally sees the senex as "the lively image of [his] grief" and takes him away to see Isabel.

Act 3, Scene 14

The Spanish King welcomes the Portuguese Viceroy with the announcement that Balthazar is betrothed to Bellamira. Will Portugal accept the marriage, scheduled to take place the following day? The Viceroy responds positively and gives up his crown on the spot: he would now like to live a solitary and religious life, ever thankful that his son is alive and well. All except the Duke and Lorenzo exit to celebrate. The Duke turns somewhat bashfully to his son and asks about his relationship to the Marshall: "It is suspected, and reported too, / That thou, Lorenzo, wrong'st Hieronimo." Given Hieronimo's importance to the King and the court in general, it would be highly undesirable for the King to hear him speak negatively of Lorenzo. Lorenzo denies any wrongdoing, despite his father's suspicion, and maintains that Hieronimo is "distract[ed] in mind" and simply mistaken. The Duke summons Hieronimo to settle the matter.

Balthazar and Bellimperia, meanwhile, are engaged in conversation. Just as the lady prudently expresses her newfound love for the prince, her father arrives. The Duke says that he has forgiven her for the affair with Andrea. Hieronimo now appears, and the Duke confronts him gently about the rumors concerning Lorenzo. Hieronimo denies vehemently any wrongdoing on Lorenzo's part, so all parties are happy and reconciled - at least on the surface.

Act 3, Scene 15

Revenge has fallen asleep, and the Ghost wakens him in alarm - it appears that Hieronimo has befriended Lorenzo! Revenge assures him that Hieronimo has not forgotten his son and stages a dumb show for his sake. The Ghost does not understand the show. Revenge explains that it represented Hymen, the god of marriage, blowing out the nuptial torches and covering them with blood.

Analysis

Following in the footsteps of his wife, Hieronimo shows clear signs of madness in the third act. When the two Portuguese men mention that they are looking for Lorenzo, Hieronimo promptly begins a rapturous speech, vividly evoking a hellish picture. His increased poetic sensibility reflects his generally heightened verbal and aural sensibilities. The mere words "son" and "murder" - not to mention the names Lorenzo and Horatio - are enough to send Hieronimo into a frenzy. In the twelfth scene of the act, for example, Hieronimo immediately picks up the ambassador's mention of his name (the question "who calls Horatio?" suggests that he is not quite within earshot) and appeals repeatedly to the king for justice. He is captive, it seems, to a deep and instinctive force.

But what, exactly, does he want? To be sure, he calls for justice and revenge - or ideally, revenge *through* justice. It is clear, however, that different forces are working within Hieronimo. His appeal for justice in front of the king begins well, but ends with him furiously digging the ground and declaring his resignation. Instead of capitalizing on the king's attention - and finally letting justice be served - Hieronimo is carried away by the desire for vengeance: "Give me my son!. . . I'll go marshal up the fiends up in hell, / To be avenged on you all for this." To the King, who cannot understand these words as well as the audience, it is as if Hieronimo is himself acting another dumb show. The King thus asks: "What means this outrage"? As the with dumb show in Act 1 Scene 5, he cannot "sound well the mystery."

Hieronimo compromises himself in front of the King and thus compromises justice as well. From the "vindicta mihi" speech in the following scene, it is clear that he has not fallen into a state of total derangement. Hieronimo still exercises enough wits to embark on a bit of Machiavellian scheming himself: he will play dumb until he finds the right moment for vengeance. One wonders, then, whether Hieronimo really desires justice - and what the word means to him. When he repeats it to the King no less than five times, he seems to call into question the very meaning of the word itself. Perhaps the scene in which he contemplates suicide can shed some light on the matter.

The opening of the twelfth scene resonates with an earlier scene in the play. It repeats, in fact, a train of thought that Hieronimo articulated Act 2 Scene 5 (in the lament that he delivers in Latin). One the one hand, he would like to join his son in death. On the other hand, he feels a need for revenge that is almost a duty, or even a categorical imperative: "Who will revenge Horatio's murder then?" As with Isabella, the thought of Horatio's murderers represents a force not complimentary, but *contrary* to the natural desire of a grieving parent. This dagger and halter capture the duality between Hieronimo's death wish and the imperative to revenge. These are the same objects used in Horatio's murder, and are thus particularly fitting for the father's suicide. At the same time, they are weapons well-suited to exacting revenge. *To be, or not to be* - critics often draw a comparison between Hamlet and Hieronimo, with good reason.

As the Marshall of Spain, the best way for Hieronimo to satisfy his need for revenge is through justice: not necessarily in the name of righteousness or the law, but as a means to an end. For Hieronimo, who has spent his life doling out justice as an official, the principle is ironically subjugated by his personal needs. When the authority of the King fails to justify the principle, Hieronimo turns to the heavens: "Ay, heaven will be revenged or every will; / Nor will they suffer murder unrepaid. / Then stay, Hieronimo, attend their will." From such a vantage point, revenge can be justified independently of authority and power. By appropriating religious principles, Hieronimo elevates himself to the same level as, say, the Viceroy, who condemns Villuppo to death. So the troubling parallel reappears once again.

Similar to Shakespeare's portrait of Hamlet, Hieronimo's character is shrouded in mystery. At times rational, at times frenzied, he traces a confusing path through the long third act of *The Spanish Tragedy*. With the poor citizens and senex in the thirteenth scene, for example, he is completely carried away by the thought of revenge and rips all the official papers presented to him. The senex's tragedy is poignantly but irrationally reduced to his own personal tragedy. Yet only one scene later, Hieronimo smoothly negotiates his treacherous act of forgiveness, seemingly in full control of his faculties. The Ghost, in any case, is fooled by Hieronimo's performance. But just as there exists a higher order of things (manifest in Revenge), appearances may not count for very much. As one nobleman put it aptly in Act 3 Scene 1, "words have several works, / And there's no credit in the countenance."

Summary and Analysis of Act 4

Act 4, Scene 1

Bellimperia berates Hieronimo for his inaction thus far: why has he neglected to avenge his son's murder? Hieronimo excuses himself, stating that he was previously unsure as to whether Bellimperia's letter contained the truth. For him, Bellimperia's desire for revenge now represents a sign from heaven: "all the saints do sit soliciting / For vengeance on those cursed murderers." He declares his resolve to exact revenge, and Bellimperia agrees to help him carry out his plot.

Balthazar and Lorenzo arrive, asking Hieronimo to provide the night's entertainment for the King. The Marshall readily agrees. A play that he wrote in his youth shall be performed - by none other than the two men, Hieronimo himself, and Bellimperia. The plot involves a knight and his wife Perseda, the Turkish emperor Soliman, and one of his Bashaws. Hoping to arrange a marriage between Soliman and Perseda, the Bashaw kills the knight. In retribution, Perseda kills Soliman and then commits suicide. Hieronimo will play the Bashaw, Balthazar will be Soliman, Lorenzo will act the knight, and Bellimperia, naturally, will play Perseda.

Balthazar calls for a comedy instead, but Hieronimo rejects the suggestion. He moreover stipulates that each character should speak in a different language. The play will thus be performed in Latin, Greek, Italian, and French. Balthazar once again objects, stating that such a mixture would only result in confusion. To this, Hieronimo promises that he will deliver an oration - and reveal a surprise - that will resolve everything in the last scene.

Act 4, Scene 2

Isabella stands at Horatio's deathplace, weapon in hand. Seeing that "neither piety nor pity moves / The king to justice or compassion," she vows to avenge herself on the very spot where her son was murdered. She cuts down the arbor where Horatio was /'/hanged and delivers a soliloquy, cursing the garden and apostrophizing Hieronimo before stabbing herself.

Act 4, Scene 3

Hieronimo enters with the Duke of Castile, who surveys Hieronimo's earnest preparations for the evening. Upon Hieronimo's request, the Duke agrees to give the king a copy of the play, as well as toss Hieronimo the key to the gallery once the royal train has entered. Balthazar passes through briefly to help with the setup. Alone on stage, Hieronimo prepares himself mentally for the evening:

> Bethink thyself, Hieronimo,
> Recall thy wits. . .

The plot is laid of dire revenge
On, then, Hieronimo, pursue revenge;
For nothing wants but acting of revenge. (IV.iii.22-30)

Act 4, Scene 4

The King arrives with the Viceroy and the Duke of Castile. The King hands the Viceroy a copy of the play, translated into English for easier understanding. The play is performed as previously summarized by Hieronimo. Hieronimo's character stabs Balthazar's, after which Bellimperia's character stabs Lorenzo's and herself. The play ends to the enthusiastic applause of the King and the Viceroy. Hieronimo then delivers the final speech: while the play may have seemed "fabulously counterfeit," he explains, it was in fact a very real spectacle. Hieronimo reveals Horatio's corpse on stage (presumably by lifting the curtains, of which he previously spoke) and declaims his accomplished revenge scheme, as well as his motives therein. Finally, "Hieronimo / Author and actor in this tragedy" runs to hang himself.

The King and the Viceroy break the locked doors and rush to detain Hieronimo. Along with the Duke of Castile, they demand to know Hieronimo's motives for orchestrating the murders. Hieronimo says in few words that he sought revenge for his son, then refuses to speak any more on the subject. The King calls for torturers, but Hieronimo bites out his tongue. The King and the Duke insist that he can still write. Hieronimo gestures for a knife to mend his pen, with he uses to stab both the Duke and himself. The King and the Viceroy exit in mourning.

Act 4, Scene 5

The Ghost declares his desires satisfied. He arranges with Revenge to have Bellimperia and Horatio treated well; in contrast, Lorenzo, Balthazar, Serberine, and Pedringano will be sent to the worst parts of hell. The two return to the underworld with Revenge's last words:

Then haste we down to meet thy friends and foes:
To place thy friends in ease, the rest in woes;
For here though death hath end their misery,
I'll there begin their endless tragedy. (IV.v.45-48)

Analysis

After the lengthy third act, almost all the loose ends of the play have been tied up. The wheel of fate is once again set in motion: all that remains is for Hieronimo's play to be staged. First, however, Isabelle commits suicide in the second scene. Readers as well as producers are faced with the question of how to interpret the scene: when she sets out to take revenge on nature, cutting down the arbor where Horatio was hanged, has she gone completely mad? Her earlier signs of lunacy suggest a positive answer. But it may be an oversimplification to reduce her actions to "madness" as such, for to do so is to bereave her suicide of rationality or meaning.

Isabella's suicide, in fact, emerges out of a logic entirely consistent with her earlier words. In Act 3 Scene 8, she expresses a longing for Horatio that is forgotten - or overridden - by her desire to find his murderers. It is unclear whether Hieronimo has told her of Lorenzo and Balthazar by the fourth act. In any case, Isabelle would be powerless to take revenge on the two young men. All she can do, then, is to "revenge [her]self upon this place" where Horatio met his untimely death. It is a gesture of protest, indeed a denial of any further life in a place that is testament to her son's death: "Fruitless for ever may this garden be, / Barren the earth." Her own suicide also can be understood in a similar manner. Apart from joining her son in death, Isabella's suicide is also designed to prevent *herself* from engendering further life: "as I curse this tree from further fruit, / So shall my womb be cursed for his sake." She, too, is part of nature; she, too, will join nature in death.

As for Hieronimo's plot, it unfolds exactly as envisioned. Just like Lorenzo, it seems, the Marshall has the gift of dissimulation and manipulation. The play itself is simple in plot, but is nonetheless intriguing. Why should it be written in four languages? Hieronimo declares at the end of the first scene: "Now shall I see the fall of Babylon, / Wrought by the heavens in this confusion." The phrase is dramatically ironic, insofar as Revenge has been working invisibly to create confusion - and doubly ironic, insofar as Revenge represents hell rather than heaven. In context, "the heavens" also points to Hieronimo himself. He has the equivalent of divine authority in the righteousness of his murder, as well as in his authorship (author derives from the Latin *auctor*, or "authority"). He is the *chef d'orchestre*, as it were.

As for the representation of Babel itself, the choice is appropriate. Babylon was one of the largest cities of the ancient world, believed to be both luxurious and corrupt. It was there that the Tower of Babel was built so high as to menace the heavens, and it was there that God punished mankind for its arrogance, spreading linguistic confusion all over the world (see Genesis 11:1-9). Balthazar and Lorenzo would make model citizens of mythical Babylon, as they are rich, powerful, and corrupt. Bellimperia herself bears the unfortunate name of Bellimperia - beautiful and powerful. They are all testament to the confusion that mankind brought upon itself through the love of wealth and power.

To the King, the play is once again like a dumb show. He requires an English translation to comprehend it, and even then he does not understand that the "fabulously counterfeit" stage is not so counterfeit after all. He cannot grasp the meaning of Horatio's corpse on stage. Just as with the dumb show in Act 1 Scene 5, Hieronimo must explain its significance - which he does at some length. But curiously, no members of the royal audience seem to understand his explanation. The King, the Viceroy, and the Duke all frantically demand to know his motives:

> *King*. Speak, traitor. . . speak!
> . . .

Vic. Why has thou murdered my Balthazar?
Cast. Why has thou butchered both my children thus?
(IV.iv.164-168.)

Hieronimo recapitulates his motives in eight lines of "good words," but even then the three men are not satisfied.

Why, then, does Hieronimo refuse to explain in greater detail the events that led up to the play-within-a-play? Perhaps his silence constitutes a form of extended revenge. The death of Horatio caused both him and his wife tremendous sufferance. By refusing to reveal the full history behind the tragic play-within-a-play, Hieronimo extends the same sufferance to the fathers of Balthazar and Lorenzo. The King, of course, does not fit into this interpretation, but Hieronimo has also gone to extremes bereft of common sense - or, for that matter, *any* sense: after biting out his tongue, he stabs the Duke of Castile before committing suicide. In one short scene, he has destroyed the future hopes of Spain and Portugal. Has justice been served? Was his revenge justified? Is revenge *ever* justified? All strife on earth, in any case, has come to an end: all characters that could potentially further the cycle of revenge have died. But as Revenge notes, the end is only the beginning of more pleasure and pain. It is up to the audience to decide whether his hell is not merely a figure for reality outside the theater.

Summary and Analysis of Anonymous Additions

Several additional scenes are printed in the 1602 edition of *The Spanish Tragedy*. They are posthumous additions, and clearly composed by a hand other than Kyd's. The first occurs between II. v. 45 and 46; the second replaces III. ii. 65 and part of 66; the third occurs between III. xi. 1 and 2; the fourth comes between III. xii and xiii; and the fifth replaces IV. iv. 169 to 192. Philip Edwards provides an authoritative gloss:

> The first, second, and last of the Additions have little commend to them; their literary quality is slight and they do much damage to Kyd's careful unfolding of plot and character. The third Addition is an imaginative piece of rhetoric which does not distort the original play; the fourth is the famous 'Painter scene' and stands head and shoulders above the rest. (lxi)

It seems that the Painter's scene, at the very least, is worth considering. But the final judgment of the additional scenes can only be passed by each individual reader, as it is altogether possible that hitherto unnoticed treasures lie in the marginal scenes.

Fourth Addition, between scenes xii and xiii

Hieronimo's two servants Jacques and Pedro enter the scene. Jacques wonders why Hieronimo has sent for them at midnight. Ever since Horatio's death, remarks Pedro, their master has been "much distraught" and "grows lunatic," sometimes apostrophizing his dead son. Hieronimo enters, searching for Horatio in the garden. He notices his servants and asks them why they have their torches lit in the dark. Despite his claims to the contrary, Hieronimo shows clear signs of madness: "Light me your torches at the mid of noon," he declares. But this is not without reason, for he bears a personal grudge against the night. In the treacherous night was Horatio killed, and if only the moon had shone, Hieronimo believes, the murderer would have seen the grace on Horatio's face and dropped the murder weapon.

Isabella enters the scene and entreats Hieronimo to return indoors. As they converse, a painter knocks on the door. Hieronimo wishes him to come and "paint some comfort." The painter, however, has his own agenda: he desires justice for the murder of his only son. Hieronimo bids everyone else leave and sits down to converse with the painter, who turns out to be the famous artist Don Bazardo. Hieronimo thus asks him whether he can paint the scene of Horatio's murder in impossible detail, with sound and movement, culminating in a frenzied request: "Make me curse, make me rave, make / me cry, make me mad, make me well again. . . and so forth." The painter agrees up until the very last and asks: "And is this the end"? At this, Hieronimo cries that "the end is death and madness!" and beats the Painter into the house. He then reemerges with a book in his hand (thus leading in to the "vindicta mihi" speech).

Analysis

In the opening of the scene, Hieronimo shows signs of madness through his inversion or confusion of such common antitheses as night and day, or sorrow and mirth. The language has a poetic quality clearly distinct from that of Kyd:

> *Hier.*Light me your torches at the mid of noon,
> Whenas the sun-god rides in all his glory:
> Light me your torches then.
> *Ped.* Then we burn daylight.
> *Hier.* Let it be burnt. (IV.ixxa.28-31)

Hieronimo's alliteration of the letter "l," which is a light enunciation that twice begins the word "light," resonates entirely inappropriately in the gloomy dark scene. He furthermore finds himself saying "we are very merry, very merry" while standing at Horatio's deathplace, much to Isabella's astonishment.

When the painter enters and expresses his desire for justice, Hieronimo offers a pithy retort: "An ounce of justice, / 'Tis a jewel so inestimable!" Don Bazardo resembles the senex Bazulto in the dramatic function that he serves. Hieronimo identifies intimately with the requests of both men, who have had their sons murdered. Both men therefore trigger a bout of madness in Hieronimo. In the painter scene's case, the effect is something of a psychological exploration. Having heard the painter's great skill in his art, Hieronimo requests a recreation of the murder scene. He makes impossible demands - realistic noise and movement, to begin with, and plenty of surrealistic detail to follow: "Let the clouds scowl, make the moon dark, the / stars extinct. . . the toads croaking, the minutes / jarring, and the clock striking twelve."

What the painter agrees to recreate is essentially Hieronimo's own vision of the fateful night. But what lies at the end of the vision? Declares Hieronimo: "O no, there is no end: the end is death and madness!" To continue along the vision, as Hieronimo has surely done many times over and over, leads to dangerous results. The painter, then, becomes a symbol of Hieronimo's imagination. He must be beaten back into the house, so as to keep "death and madness" at bay.

Suggested Essay Questions

1. The Spanish General, Lorenzo, and Horatio all tell different stories about the battle. What actually happened? The question may be fruitless in itself, but it leads to a more interesting question: What motivates their narrative? In other words, why do the different characters tell the versions that they do?
2. Discuss the role of the Chorus (the Ghost and Revenge) in the play. What does it suggest about fate and human agency? It may be helpful to approach the question from the play's "theatricality," or alternatively Hieronimo's belief that he is serving justice due in Heaven.
3. Why does Hieronimo delay taking his revenge for so long? Each time someone says "Horatio" or "murder," it is as if he recalls anew the need for revenge. Consider the question in relation to his spells of madness as well as his death wishes.
4. What does the sub-plot that occurs in Portugal (i.e. Villuppo's treachery and its resolution) add to the play? Can it be understood allegorically, or does it contain insightful parallels to the rest of the play?
5. Perform a close reading of the dialogue between Bellimperia, Balthazar, and Lorenzo in Act 3 Scene 10. Lines 78-109, in particular, culminate in an obscure exchange about love and fear. Students of Latin are encouraged to pay special attention to Bellimperia's two lines 102-103.
6. Hieronimo demands justice for Horatio's murder. Has justice been served at the end of the play? How does justice overlap with revenge, and how are the two different?
7. Discuss the different modes of suicide in the play. Why do Isabelle, Hieronimo, and Bellimperia kill themselves? Does a common motive exist between the three?
8. Consider the portrait of madness in the play. What are its symptoms? How does it arise? Can it be distinguished between masculine and feminine forms - between Hieronimo and Isabella?
9. Discuss the significance of the play-within-play in the fourth act. Why does Hieronimo insist on showing Horatio's corpse on stage? Why must it be acted out in four different languages? It may also be worthwhile to consider it in relation to the dumb shows that occur in the play.
10. After the play-within-a-play, the royal audience does not seem to comprehend Hieronimo's explanation of his motives for killing Lorenzo and Balthazar. They insist repeatedly that he speak and explain himself again. How might this lack of comprehension be understood? And why does Hieronimo refuse to speak anymore?
11. The murder of the Duke comes as a complete surprise. The turn of events (with Hieronimo being restrained from hanging himself and thus biting off his tongue) strongly suggest that the murder is not premeditated. Has Hieronimo simply gone completely mad? What role does the murder serve in the larger picture of the play?

Marginalia of The Spanish Tragedy

For writers of the Elizabethan and Jacobean theater, it was standard practice to introduce foreign phrases where appropriate. Both as a return to classicism and as a second language to the educated, Latin was particularly popular. The extent of the usage of non-English varied between authors. Christopher Marlowe and Ben Jonson, for example, were generally more heavy-handed than William Shakespeare. As for Thomas Kyd, he certainly did not hesitate to incorporate Latin in *The Spanish Tragedy*. The not insignificant amount of Latin in the play has, from Kyd's time, been often seen as an intrusion on the stage, and hence a weakness. Arthur Freeman notes that critics have also been "seized upon to ridicule Kyd's pedantry" (83). Most audiences at the time, however, would have not have been entirely alienated by the occasional Latin or Latinate phrases.

For many modern readers and audiences, non-English phrases are consigned to the margins. Hardly any phrases more sophisticated than "E tu, Brute?" are understood by a general audience. At the theater, the ear skips easily over an unfamiliar phrase; while scanning a page, the eye may or may not glance at the marginal translation. The marginalia are often neglected - and unjustly so. As a methodical examination of *The Spanish Tragedy* will show, marginalia have their own history, often richer than that of the main text. This history is particularly welcoming to readers of a play (as opposed to spectators, who do not have the luxury of examining the passages at their leisure).

One of the most interesting readings of *The Spanish Tragedy* centers around three Senecan quotations in Act 3 Scene 8. Eminent theatrical historian Scott McMillan returns to an old question among scholars: how does one explain Hieronimo's clear misuse of Seneca in his "Vindica mihi" speech? To pass it off as an accident or as Kyd's poor knowledge of Latin, argues McMillan, would constitute a "critical negligence" (201). In McMillan's reading, Hieronimo himself becomes a reader:

> [Hieronimo] is not "caught" in the ironic position of Clytemnestra, Andromache, and Oedipus. . . He has, in a way, mastered this irony. . . and in locating three Senecan characters caught in the situation which he has mastered, *he bends their lines to his purpose* because he knows that situation better than they and means to enact it. (207, italics mine)

Only a select few readers or spectators - in both Kyd's time and today - would be able to first understand the Latin, then identify its source, and finally recall its context. McMillan's reading shows that an archaeological trip into the marginalia of plays can yield fruitful results, and suggests that many treasures may lay yet undiscovered.

The notes to A. K. McIlwraith's edition of The Spanish Tragedy have been quoted for the translations from the Latin. R. S. Boas's notes, as well as those of FÃ©lix CarÃ¨rre, have supplied the allusions and references.

Act 1

I. ii. 12-14. An adaptation from the court-poet Claudian's *De Tertio Consulatu Honorii*, 96-98.

O multum dilecte Deo, tibi militat aether,
Et conjuratae curvato poplite gentes
Succumbunt; recti soror est victoria juris

O well-beloved of God, the heavens fight for thee,
And spell-bound peoples fall on bended knee [sic];
For victory is sister of true right.

I. ii. 55-56. The lines seem to be taken partly from the Roman poet Statius's *Thebais*, viii. 399 and molded on an analogy like that found in Virgil's *The Aeneid*, x. 361. Here the Latin is more terse and economical than an equivalent phrase in English.

Pede pes et cuspide cuspis;
Arma sonant armis, vir petiturque viro.

Foot against foot, lance against lance is thrust,
Arms clash on arms, man is attacked by man.

I. iii. 15-17. Probably a mixed adaptation: similar versions of the first line are quoted proverbially by some authors contemporary to Kyd, and the remaining two lines are close to Seneca's *Agamemnon*, 698-698:

Qui jacet in terra, non habet unde cadat.
In me consumpsit vires fortuna nocendo
Nil superest ut jam possit obesse magis.

He who is prostrate hath no where to fall.
Fortune hath spent her force for ill on me:
Greater disaster cannot be in store.

Act 2

II. i. 41. An Italian phrase meaning "come here quickly" (in its modern form "vieni qui presto").

Vien qui presto.

II. i. 107. A well-known Latin motto.

tam armis quam ingenio.

by force as well as wile.

II. v. 67-80. A pastiche of allusions, quotes, and Kyd's own composition. Lines 72-73 resemble a passage from the Roman poet Tibullus, ii. 4. 55 ff., and the phrase "sic, sic juvat ire sub umbras" in line 78 quotes *The Aeneid*, iv. 660. An interesting antithesis occurs between the herbs of "fair spring" and the "fatal poison[ous]" herbs, as both are equally desired for their potential to alleviate Hieronimo's pain. In the perverse world of murder and revenge, perhaps, typical values have been overthrown. Hieronimo's desire for death so as to never again see his dead son is also ironic, given the presence of the spectre/spectators Ghost and Revenge, who come into the scene immediately afterwards.

O aliquis mihi quas pulchrum ver educat herbas
. . .
Ne mortem vindicta tuam tam nulla sequatur.

Compound for me all herbs that the fair spring
Brings forth, to serve as salve unto my pain;
Or bring me blossoms of oblivion.
Myself will garner all fell seeds the sun
Draws to the shores of light, and I will drink
All venoms any sorceress can devise,
And all the fatal poisons herbs provide;
I will essay all these, until at once
All senses perish in my dying breast.-
So then shall I ne'er see thy face, dear son,
And shall eternal darkness cover thee?
With thee I die: thus would I pass the bourne.-
No, no! I will not yield my life so soon,
Lest so thy death should lack its due revenge.

Act 3

III. ii. 94. An unintelligible phrase. *ieron* in Greek is the *ieros*, which means "sacred" or "a sacred place." The phrase seen as a mixture of Italian and Greek could potentially be understood as "what a sacred place"-an ironic reference to the park where Pedringano will kill Serberine. Such an interpretation remains far-fetched.

Che le Ieron!

III. iv. 87-88. An Italian phrase.

E quel che voglio io, nessun lo sa;
Intendo io: quel mi bastere

And that which I want, none knows;
I intend, which will suffice for me.

III. x. 102-103. A Latin phrase of uncertain origin; its meaning in context is also unclear.

Et tremolo metui pavidum junxere timorum,
Et vanum stolidae proditionis opus.

They joined to trembling fright a quivering fear,
A futile act of blockish self-betrayal.

III. xiii. 1, 6, 11-12, 35. Hieronimo enters the scene carrying a book; judging from the quotations that appear in the passage, it is a book of Seneca. Line 1 quotes Octavia, a play traditionally attributed to Seneca; line 6 quotes *Agamemmnon*, 115; lines 11-12 quote *Troades*, 510-512; and line 35 quotes *Oedipus*, 515.

Vindicta Mihi!

Revenge is due to me!

Per scelus semper tutum est sceleribus iter.

Through crime is ever the safe way for crime.

Fata si miseros juvant, habes salutem:
Fata si vitam negant, habes sepulchrum

If Fates befriend a wretch, thou hast a refuge;
If Fates deny thee life, thou hast a tomb.

Remedium malorum iners est.

It is an idle remedy for ills.

III. xiii. 62. Boas writes: "A writ which lay to eject a tenant from his holding" (408).

ejectione firmae

III. xiv. 118. Boas notes that this Spanish phrase meaning "few words" became a "stock jest" after Kyd's use here (118). Shakespeare quotes it in *The Taming of The Shrew*, Induction, 5.

pocas palabris

III. xiv. 168-169. An Italian phrase, printed variously depending on the edition. The essential meaning is: "He who unexpectedly befriends me wishes to betray me."

Chi mi fa pie carezze che non suole,
Tradito mi ha, o tradir mi vuole.

Who caresses more than was his way
Has betrayed me, or wishes to betray me.

Act 4

IV.i.159. A tragedy done in lofty style; *cothurnata* means "wearing the buskin," a boot which Athenian tragic actors wore.

Tragedia cothurnata

Author of ClassicNote and Sources

Taro Kuriyama, author of ClassicNote. Completed on July 24, 2007, copyright held by GradeSaver.

Updated and revised Jordan Berkow August 27, 2007. Copyright held by GradeSaver.

Felix Carre. *Le Theatre de Thomas Kyd; contribution a l'atitude du drame Elizabethain.* Toulouse: E. Privat, 1951.

Phillip Edwards. "Introduction" in Thomas Kyd, *The Spanish Tragedy*. Cambridge: Harvard University Press, 1959.

Arthur Freeman. *Thomas Kyd: Facts and Problems.* London: Oxford University Press, 1967.

Thomas Kyd. *The Spanish Tragedy* in Five Elizabethan Tragedies. Ed. A. K. McIlwraith. Westport, CT: Greenwood Press, 1981.

Thomas Kyd. *The Works of Thomas Kyd.* Ed. F. S. Boas. London: Oxford University Press, 1967.

Scott McMillan. "The Book of Seneca in The Spanish Tragedy." *Studies in English Literature*. 14. 2 (1974): 201-208. JSTOR. Harvard University Libaries. 19 July 2007. <http://www.jstor.org>.

Peter B. Murray. *Thomas Kyd.* New York: Twayne Publishers, Inc., 1969.

Virgil. *The Aeneid* in *The Longman Anthology of World Literature.* Vol. A. Trans. Robert Fitzgerald. Pearson Education, Inc., 2004. 1167-1259.

Essay: ENDINGS IN RENAISSANCE TRAGEDY

by Prateek Swaika
June 18, 2006

Among the various definitions of tragedy, the one most commonly proffered is: a play that treats - at the most uncompromising level - human suffering, or pathos, with death being the usual conclusion. According to Aristotle's Poetics, the purpose of tragedy is to show how humans are at the mercy of fate, and to cleanse the audience by provoking extreme emotions of pity and terror. The tragic actions on the dramatic stage cause the audience to experience these extreme feelings that eventually causes a catharsis or release of these emotions, to reduce these passions to a healthy, balanced proportion.

However, the application of this definition to Renaissance tragedy is limited as it makes two over reaching assumptions about the play, its protagonists and the audience. First, that the death of all protagonists contributing towards the drama is tragic to an equal degree, which prompts an equal level of catharsis in the audience. Does the self-purchased death of one simultaneously learned and overly ambitious Faustus solicit the same amount of catharsis and empathy as do the 'unnecessary' deaths of Cordelia, Gloucester, Lear, the Duke of Castile, Horatio, and Isabel among a host of other innocent characters whose corpses litter the sets of King Lear and The Spanish Tragedy? One is left with a terrifying uncertainty - although the iniquitous die, the good die along with them. Second, and perhaps most significant, that catharsis would pour forth in the audience if the play's dÃ©nouement - meaningful or not - contains fatal twists, surprise deaths and wide-scale massacre. Or in other words, though the play may itself may have physically ended, the repercussions of the deaths, its implied message on human fate and deeper unresolved, psychological issues that had plagued the protagonists' minds continue to trouble audiences long after they have left the theatres.

The deaths of Lear and Cordelia in King Lear confront us like a raw, fresh wound when our every instinct calls for healing and reconciliation. This problem, moreover, is as much one of philosophic order as of dramatic effect. In what sort of universe, we ask ourselves, can wasteful death follow suffering and torture? If characters such as Lear, Gloucester, and Edmund all go through a process of awakening, why then do they die? Even Iago, despite all his evil machinations, lives on to bear the fruit of his crimes. In other Shakespearean tragedies, such as Othello and Hamlet, the play ends with the reconciliation of the tragic hero and society. When Othello pleads "Speak of me as I am. Nothing extenuate, /Nor set down aught in malice," like Hamlet and Cleopatra he seeks immortality in his reputation and in his story. It is a final attempt to reconcile himself with society and his misdeeds, moments before he stabs himself.

In Romeo and Juliet, there is a feeling of hope in the final scene because the Houses of Montague and Capulet are finally at peace with each other, and will erect monuments in remembrance of the two lovers. Peace and understanding is gained from the tragedy. But in The Spanish Tragedy the only monument we see is that of a pile of dead bodies slumped behind a curtain. It is difficult at the end, for the audience to feel whether anything has been gained other than a sense of remorse and misery.

In a Christian framework, even the worst deed can be forgiven through the redemptive power of Christ. Thus, however terrible Faustus' pact with Lucifer may be, the possibility of redemption is always open to him. But each time the play offers moments in which Faustus can choose to repent, he decides to remain loyal to Lucifer rather than seek heaven. "Christ did call the thief upon the cross," he comforts himself, referring to the New Testament story of the thief who was crucified alongside Jesus Christ, repented for his sins, and was promised a place in paradise. That he compares himself to this figure shows that Faustus assumes he can wait until the last moment and still escape hell. In other words, he wants to renounce Mephistopheles, but not just yet. One can easily anticipate that his willingness to delay will prove fatal. Only at the end of his life does Faustus desire to repent, and, in the final scene, he cries out to Christ to redeem him. But it is too late for him to repent. In creating this moment in which Faustus is still alive but incapable of being redeemed, Marlowe steps outside the Christian worldview in order to maximize the dramatic power of the final scene. Having inhabited a Christian world for the entire play, Faustus spends his final moments in a slightly different universe, where redemption is no longer possible and where certain sins can no longer be forgiven.

The effect of inhabiting such an unforgiving universe before his death is however ameliorated in later versions of the text. The ending of the Doctor Faustus B text is vastly different to that of the A text. The latter simply ends with Faustus being dragged away by the devils, and a summarising epilogue. Nothing is revealed to the audience of what eventually becomes of his body. The B Text however is slightly more re-assuring. Despite his self-aggrandisement, wavering, "hair-splitting, and sophomoric misquotations of the Scriptures," Faustus gets a sympathetic ear to listen to his agonized confession of his pact with Lucifer, and subsequently "a due burial" from the scholars. His scattered limbs are gathered by the scholars, who promise him a burial in accordance with Christian rights, "though Faustus' end be such." Unlike Don Andreas in The Spanish Tragedy, proper burial rites will buy Faustus a ride in Charon's boat across the Styx to Hades. King Lear's death, in comparison, breaks all dramatic conventions. It is perhaps one of the few tragedies in which the tragic hero dies irreconciled and indifferent to society.

The last two acts of King Lear are constructed with a series of advances and repudiations of visions of hope. By choosing to set King Lear in a pre-Christian era, markedly before Christ's redemption, Shakespeare does not allow one the comfort of knowing that all evil, however bad, can be overcome. Nature seems to be mocking Edgar's confidence in justice, when he sees his brutally blinded father immediately after claiming that "the worst is not / So long as we can say 'this is the worst."

In Hamlet, a play equally wrenched by a self-consuming family quarrel, Horatio bears witness to the ensuing tragedy. In the closing scene, he volunteers to go outside and narrate to the world the misfortunes that have befallen this once noble family. He will reveal all the "carnal, bloody, and unnatural acts" as well as the "accidental judgements" and "casual slaughters" so that men may learn from their mistakes. Hamlet's audience is thus awarded with some release after this gut-wrenching tragedy. The world will be informed that Hamlet was a just man. But what will the world think of Lear? Albeit a symbolic act, no one will tell his story, and in a way, purge oneself of further adversity. Hence, a strong sense of guilt and remorse, what in truth ought to have been the burden of the remaining characters, is instead passed onto the audience to bear.

But that does not seem to be happening in King Lear, The Spanish Tragedy or Doctor Faustus. Not one steps forward to offer any words of closure or perhaps a glimpse of optimism. Kyd's decision to literally give Revenge the last word in his play reflects the thematic message of the final scenes of The Spanish Tragedy: revenge does have the last word, crowding out mercy and all other human emotions, seeking its inexorable satisfaction in an overdose bloodshed and violence. The final scene implies that Hieronimo's action serves as the fulfillment of justice, but the blood, waste, and carnage of the penultimate scene works against this presumption, seeming to deny the possibility of justice in a world where the machinations of class and power determine the course of men's lives.

In King Lear, Edgar simply offers, "Speak what we feel, not what we ought to say." Though sensible, his comment is untimely for indeed had this maxim been observed by everyone and not just by Cordelia and Kent, perhaps the tragedy could have been averted. It is perhaps for these reasons that Tolstoy refers to the plot of King Lear to be "stupid, verbose, unnatural, unintelligible, bombastic, vulgar, tedious, and full of incredible events, 'wild ravings', 'mirthless jokes', anachronisms, irrelevancies, obscenities, worn-out stage conventions and other faults both moral and aesthetic. " This could well have been a view shared by Nahum Tate which made him revert closer to Shakespeare's sources, in terms of the dÃ©nouement.

Texts such as Holinshed's Chronicles, which Shakespeare had at his elbow when he wrote his history-plays, end in the reconciliation of a father whom submits his daughters to a 'love-test'. Shakespeare's choice therefore, to end the play in such ghoulish bloodshed can be seen as a clear attempt to point out the weakness of humankind, and the evil it is capable of. In King Lear, Shakespeare does not merely adapt his sources, he consciously makes a violent and shocking alteration to them. He converts the folk-tales of medieval literature into a more complex account, where everything is obfuscated and questionable, in a manner similar to the dÃ©nouement itself. (Hieronimo is at least partly aware, and quick to exploit the inability of audiences to comprehend such large-scale tragedies when he chooses to perform his play in a medley of foreign languages, the effect of which Balthazar rightly notes,

"...this will be a mere confusion/ And hardly shall we be all understood.")

The deaths in Hamlet are curiously unrelated to the demands of the Ghost. And the latter, unlike tradition, does not return to haunt the stage at the end to revel in the deaths not in the dubiously-gained revenge. Hamlet's decision not to kill Claudius is indeed a thoughtful mistake, a missed opportunity that would not only have ended the play in less than half the time, preventing the deaths of so many people, but would have also earned him his revenge rightfully. While Hieronimo proceeds to his last rendezvous in as an agent of death in a deliberate manner ("And princes, now behold Hieronimo, /Author and actor in this tragedy."). Hamlet almost stumbles on his final best chance to kill Claudius as a consequence of a duel with Laertes and various plots of poison that he knew nothing of previously, so that his final act of killing is almost knee-jerk and prompted by self-defence rather than planned strategy.

Unlike in Hamlet, in The Spanish Tragedy the choric Don Andreas is quick to take centre-stage and revel in the carnage. With only the promise of an afterlife presided over by Pluto and Proserpina, the dÃ©nouement has nakedly pagan overtones and no sign of completeness. Not only was Don Andreas able to destroy the lives of his enemies while they were living, but also after they are dead. In a frenzy of blood-lust, he demands and gets the authority to provide everlasting judgement for his rivals. Here, there is no end to the incessant pain - the revenge, and therefore the play, continues to perpetuity. Lorenzo has been confined eternally on Ixion's wheel; Castile is to have his liver perpetually torn at by vultures, and Balthazar is to be hung about Chimaera's neck.

Hieronimo acknowledges the tragedian's 'faked endings' when he notes:

To die today, for fashioning our scene,

The death of Ajax, or some Roman peer,

And in a minute starting up again,

Revive to please tomorrow's audience.

While a tragedy suggests a certain irreversible finality in the catastrophic events of the play - an irrevocability that is integral to the audience feeling the catharsis - at the end of the day, it is simply and subversively, a play. Dead actors rise up once more, wipe off the pig's blood, and reappear on stage again the following day. In real terms, for the audience, it perhaps wasn't such a 'tragic end' after all.

Many critics have not just disapproved of the deaths of Lear and Cordelia, but have also expressed concerns with the implausibility in the plot. Among the host of 'dramatic defects' that Bradley points out in King Lear, the one that remains the most jarring of them all is Edmund's long delay in telling of his 'writ' on the lives of

Cordelia and Lear even after he is mortally wounded and has nothing to gain. Stemming from it is yet the biggest war on the senses. Albany's most unbelievable forgetfulness ("Great thing of us forgot") is widely seen by critics as the greatest injustice in the play. For the "loving son of Albany" (who is soon also to take up the rein of power in Britain) to overlook, albeit in the midst of Goneril and Regan's deaths, the safety of the unwell King and Cordelia, is inexplicable. If we are to remind ourselves of Albany's prior knowledge of Edmund's diabolical capabilities and the latter's arrest "on capital treason," then to suggest that Albany did not suspect Lear and Cordelia's lives to be in danger, makes his forgetfulness seem even more implausible.

Renaissance dramatists explore the limits of human justice and leave us with doubts about any other form of justice. One may feel that the dÃ©nouements with their varying degrees of penalties are not quite fair, even though all sinners have been punished. Goneril, Regan, Balthazar, Lorenzo and their collaborators are as dead as Macbeth or Richard III, but so are Cordelia and Bel-imperia, and with them, innocence and hope for the future. No number of slain villains can alleviate the accumulated devastation. Perhaps Horatio's fate ought to have been better than that of a low-life such as Pedringano, and perhaps Goneril and Regan ought to have remained alive in order to witness a happy reunion between Lear and Cordelia. In illustrating this unpredictable hand of justice, both human and divine, the dramatists illustrate the worst features of mankind at work, and in doing so, invite one to react and remain uncomfortable towards any suggestion of a resolution.

BIBLIOGRAPHY:

Â Bevington, D. and Rasmussen, E.: Introduction to the OUP edition of Christopher Marlowe: Doctor Faustus and Other Plays

Â Bevington, D: Introduction to the MUP edition of The Spanish Tragedy

Â Bradbrook, M.C.; Themes and Conventions of Elizabethan Tragedy

Â Bradley, A.C.; Shakespearean Tragedy

Â Foakes, R.A.; Introduction to the Arden Shakespeare Edition of King Lear

Â Mack, Maynard; Actors and Redactors (1965)

Â Mangan, Michael; A preface to Shakespeare's Tragedies

Â Orwell, George; Lear, Tolstoy and the Fool (1950)

Â Stampfer, J.C; The Catharsis of King Lear

Essay: "Just and Sharp Revenge": The Question of Underworld Justice in "The Spanish Tragedy"

by Jenna Weiner
February 22, 2007

"'Send him,' quoth [Minos], 'to our infernal king, / To doom him as best seems his majesty" (1.1.52-3). Nestled in the lengthy opening monologue by Don Andrea, these lines introduce the overarching question that Thomas Kyd's The Spanish Tragedy seeks to answer - the question of Don Andrea's "doom." In the underworld, Aeacus and Rhadamanth argue about Don Andrea's fate, about whether he should spend his eternity "walk[ing] with lovers in our fields of love," or if he "must to martial fields" (1.1.42, 47). While Don Andrea's role in the play can easily be overlooked for the revenge plots taking place among the living characters, his importance should not be minimized. Don Andrea serves as the instigator and the Chorus for the revenge plots, which are all under the heading of his own revenge. Yet, if he is so important, why can't the underworld decide where he should spend eternity? Many episodes in the play suggest that the underworld operates as an inefficient system. The question is thus one of Kyd's intentions: The Spanish Tragedy is either a well-intentioned but unflattering portrayal of the underworld, or a deliberate statement of its inefficiency. By questioning and exploring the fairness and efficiency of the underworld, this essay argues that the conflict surrounding Don Andrea's fate positions the play as a critique of the dominant conception of the afterlife in sixteenth-century England.

The most problematic representation of justice in the underworld occurs at the end of the play, when Don Andrea sentences all of his friends and enemies to their fates in the underworld. He asks if "he may consort [his] friends in pleasing sort,/ And on [his] foes work just and sharp revenge" and states his desire to "be judge and doom them to unrest" (4.5.15-6, 29-30). While the play is centered upon Don Andrea's quest for revenge, it is unclear who or what gives him the authority to decide the fates of others, particularly the fates of those who were not involved in his death. While his acts against the characters who were directly involved in his death are legible as acts of revenge, it is less clear why Don Andrea assumes authority over the fates of those uninvolved. Kyd thus represents underworld justice as a system that is not based on impartiality: no character makes any objective judgment about the relationship between the characters' morality and their eternal doom. When Don Andrea details how he will bestow "sweet pleasure to eternal days" on Bel-Imperia, Isabella, and Hieronimo (who commit murder, suicide, and both, respectively) and after he sadistically explains (in gruesome detail) his plan to damn the rest, Revenge simply assents, stating "then haste we down to meet thy friends and foes:/ To place thy friends in ease, the rest in woes" (4.5.24, 45-6). He assigns himself to execute Don Andrea's will, without any evidence of ensuring the righteousness of his judgement.

The play also calls into question the relationship between justice and revenge. Why is Don Andrea even allowed to avenge his death at all? Why is he sent to Revenge? The text's main justification is that Don Andrea's death was itself unjust, caused by "young Don Balthazar with ruthless rage,/ Taking advantage of his foe's distress" (1.4.23-4). It may be relevant that Andrea was briefly prevented from entering the underworld as a result of his "rites of burial not performed" in a timely way, but later, Horatio gives a touching account of how he buried his dear friend (1.1.21). The only apparent objection to the justice of Andrea's death is that Don Balthazar was unsportsmanlike in the murder. However, one must remember that Andrea's death was on the battlefield, where everyone participates in conscious anticipation of their own murder. Andrea, after all, was not ambushed and killed as Horatio was, or even secretly poisoned as are so many characters in revenge plays. Andrea knew the stakes.

The ambiguity surrounding Don Andrea's fate compels readers to question the efficiency and utility of the underworld system. As Kyd's sixteeth-century audience would expect to see the underworld depicted as the legitimate reality of the afterlife, it is provocative that the play presents the process of justice in the underworld as based on flimsy, even flippant judgements. For example, Pluto allowed Don Andrea's fate to be decided by Proserpine, when she "begged that only she might give [Don Andrea his] doom," to which "Pluto was pleased, and sealed it with a kiss" (1.1.79-80). The inherent foolishishness of the scenario - Pluto determining a man's fate according to his lover's fancy - casts doubt on the legitimacy of the underworld. How could such an indecisive and somewhat arbitrary system be functional?

It is also significant that the roles Don Andrea occupies - a lover and a soldier - are not mutually exclusive. Yet, Kyd presents that duality as enough to cause confusion and indecision in the underworld, leaving Don Andrea without a determined fate. When "the manner of [Don Andrea's] life and death" was discussed, Minos describes that he "both lived and died in love,/ And for his love tried fortune of the wars,/ And by war's fortune lost both love and life," after which Rhadamanth and Aeacus argue over different interpretations (1.1.37-40). Could something as unremarkable as coexisting as a lover and a soldier be enough to unravel the system of the underworld? Of course, the argument between Rhadamanth and Aeacus over Don Andrea's fate is not proof that his fate cannot be decided, for they did decide to send him to Pluto for sentencing. Yet the fact that Pluto does not take the decision seriously and allows Proserpine's whim to decide his fate, as well as the fact that Don Andrea's fate is still undisclosed at the end of the play implies that Don Andrea's fate is in fact uncertain. The underworld is unable to understand Don Andrea's character because he occupies the role of lover and fighter simultaneously. How can anyone's fate be decided in such black and white terms? That this question is what fuels the conflict over Don Andrea's fate suggests that Kyd undermines the concept of underworld justice by portraying it as an inefficient method of determining one's eternal fate.

The structure of the play itself alludes to the imperfection of the underworld. In particular, the play presents revenge as devastating and never-ending. For most of the characters, "though death hath end their misery,/ [Revenge will] there begin their endless tragedy" (4.5.47-8). That Don Andrea's appetite for revenge is allowed to determine the fates of so many characters raises the possibility of an infinite regress. If Don Andrea can doom other characters after (and because of) his death, it follows that each character that dies will be given their own power to exact revenge in the afterlife, a situation which could lead to mass death and destruction. The plot of the play, therefore, depends on the idea of revenge as destructive and infinite - after all, revenge causes the death of most of the characters - yet the eternal fates of these characters are decided by their own vengeful behavior. The implication is that the underworld is unethical nature. By allowing the characters' fates to be determined only by their actions in the revenge plot, their fates are reduced to nothing more than the likes and dislikes of Revenge and a vengeful Ghost. By allowing revenge - a concept that the play has established as destructive - determine the fates of the characters, Kyd undermines the ethical integrity of the underworld. In contrast to the religious, virtue-based afterlives that are the alternatives, it seems unlikely that Kyd would have endorsed a system that determines the fates of souls based on vicious revenge.

Could Kyd's criticism be directed at revenge, and not the underworld as a whole? The play-within-a-play, "Soloman and Perseda," represents revenge that is executed through trickery and deceit. The play places a distinct emphasis on confusion and chaos: staged in four different languages, "Solomon and Perseda" alludes to the Tower of Babel - a biblical allegory that explains the discord between human groups. It is discord that also fuels revenge. The play illustrates the immoral and damaging nature of revenge. The mere fact that mortal revenge is not enough - that revenge extends into the afterlife - speaks to the unquenchable sadism of revenge itself and vengeful mortals. Yet, we must ask, why is the most vengeful character - Don Andrea - allowed to be the decisive, authoritative figure in the play? If the play is a criticism of revenge, Don Andrea would be the most damned of all. Yet in terms of his eternal fate, he seems to be the most privileged among the dead. Kyd uses his critique of revenge to demonstrate the injustice of the underworld.

Ultimately, the unjust nature of the underworld in The Spanish Tragedy reflects a deep pessimism that permeates the play's action. After all, Kyd does not posit an alternative to the system of fate-decision in the mythic underworld. Perhaps The Spanish Tragedy's underworld represents the flawed system of human justice; perhaps Kyd does not believe in any afterlife. In either case, the instances of injustice in the underworld indicate that our lives and fates may very well be determined by a force that is arbitrary and unjust, if determined by anything at all. The corresponding clichÃ©, of course, is that fate is blind. The world that Kyd constructs in The Spanish Tragedy - a world full of treachery, bloodthirsty avengers, murder and deceit - suggests a rather bleak version of reality, in both life and the afterlife. If life can be so unjust, Kyd suggests, the eternal fate of humanity might be just as hopeless.

Works Cited

Kyd, Thomas. The Spanish Tragedie. Ed. Emma Smith. London: Penguin Books, 1998.

Quiz 1

1. **Who was Don Andrea?**
   A. A Portuguese nobleman
   B. A Portuguese courtier
   C. A Spanish general
   D. A Spanish courtier

2. **Who killed Don Andrea?**
   A. Horatio
   B. The Portuguese Viceroy
   C. Balthazar
   D. Alexandro

3. **Who performed Andrea's last rites?**
   A. Horatio
   B. Lorenzo
   C. Balthazar
   D. Bellimperia

4. **Which of the judges of Hades sends Andrea to see Pluto?**
   A. Rhadamanth
   B. Proserpine
   C. Aecus
   D. Minos

5. **Who passes Andrea's final judgment?**
   A. Revenge
   B. Proserpine
   C. Minos
   D. Pluto

6. **Through which gate do Andrea and Revenge pass to leave the underworld?**
   A. The gates of gold
   B. The gates of horn
   C. The gates of iron
   D. The gates of ivory

7. **What does Revenge predict in the induction to the play?**
    A. Hieronimo will kill Balthazar
    B. Bellimperia will kill Balthazar
    C. The Duke of Castile will die
    D. Horatio will be killed by Lorenzo

8. **What does the King reward the Spanish General with?**
    A. Nothing
    B. His chain
    C. His sword
    D. Ten ducats

9. **What is the official status between Portugal and Spain, according to the Spanish General?**
    A. Continued belligerence
    B. Peace conditional
    C. Peace
    D. No official status

10. **What is the reward that the King grants each soldier?**
    A. Ten ducats
    B. Two ducats
    C. A gram of gold
    D. A chain

11. **Who brings Balthazar to see the King?**
    A. Horatio alone
    B. Lorenzo alone
    C. Lorenzo and Balthazar
    D. The Spanish General

12. **Who is Balthazar?**
    A. The Portuguese Viceroy's son
    B. A Portuguese nobleman
    C. Lorenzo's brother
    D. A former Spanish courtier

13. **Who gets custody of Balthazar?**
    A. Horatio
    B. Lorenzo
    C. Hieronimo
    D. The Duke of Castile

14. **What official title does Hieronimo hold?**
    A. General
    B. Captain
    C. Marshall
    D. None

15. **Who receives the reward for capturing Balthazar?**
    A. The reward is buried with Andrea's body
    B. Both Horatio and Lorenzo
    C. Horatio only
    D. Lorenzo only

16. **What does the Viceroy lament above all when he first appears on stage?**
    A. His son's death
    B. The death of his general
    C. Portugal's defeat
    D. The loss of Portugal's fortunes

17. **What does Villuppo claim that Alexandro did?**
    A. He shot Balthazar in the back
    B. He stabbed Baltazar in the back
    C. He shot Andrea in battle
    D. He attempted to flee the battlefield

18. **On what basis does Viceroy confirm Villuppo's accusation against Alexandro?**
    A. Based on what he saw in battle
    B. Based on his dream
    C. Based on a soldier's claim
    D. Based on his imagination

19. **What gesture does the Viceroy make when he accuses Alexandro of treachery?**
    A. He thrusts his sword in the air
    B. He throws his chain at Alexandro
    C. He takes off his crown and puts it back on
    D. He slams his scepter on the ground

20. **For what does Villuppo betray Alexandro?**
    A. For fame
    B. For the sake of pure villainy
    C. For a reward
    D. For revenge

21. **What does Horatio retrieve from Andrea's corpse?**
    A. A sword
    B. A portrait
    C. A chain
    D. A scarf

22. **To what does Horatio attribute Andrea's fall in battle?**
    A. Balthazar's strength
    B. The goddess Nemesis's intervention
    C. Andrea's weakness
    D. Pure circumstance

23. **What does Bellimperia drop that Horatio picks up?**
    A. A glove
    B. A diamond
    C. A ring
    D. A scarf

24. **Who orchestrates the first masque?**
    A. A clown
    B. The Duke
    C. Lorenzo
    D. Hieronimo

25. **What does the first masque represent?**

A. Three knights fighting each other

B. Three knights submitting to three kings

C. Three kings exchanging their coat of arms

D. Three knights conquering three kings

Quiz 1 Answer Key

1. **(D)** A Spanish courtier
2. **(C)** Balthazar
3. **(A)** Horatio
4. **(D)** Minos
5. **(B)** Proserpine
6. **(B)** The gates of horn
7. **(B)** Bellimperia will kill Balthazar
8. **(B)** His chain
9. **(B)** Peace conditional
10. **(B)** Two ducats
11. **(C)** Lorenzo and Balthazar
12. **(A)** The Portuguese Viceroy's son
13. **(B)** Lorenzo
14. **(C)** Marshall
15. **(B)** Both Horatio and Lorenzo
16. **(A)** His son's death
17. **(A)** He shot Balthazar in the back
18. **(B)** Based on his dream
19. **(C)** He takes off his crown and puts it back on
20. **(C)** For a reward
21. **(D)** A scarf
22. **(B)** The goddess Nemesis's intervention
23. **(A)** A glove
24. **(D)** Hieronimo
25. **(D)** Three knights conquering three kings

Quiz 2

1. **Which knight is not mentioned in the first masque?**
   A. The Duke of Edinburgh
   B. The Duke of Lancaster
   C. The Earl of Gloucester
   D. The Earl of Kent in Albion

2. **To whom does the King drink at the first banquet?**
   A. Horatio
   B. The ambassador
   C. Hieronimo
   D. The Viceroy

3. **Why is the Ghost displeased after the first act?**
   A. The King has not properly recognized his achievment in battle
   B. Bellimperia has betrayed him
   C. Balthazar is enjoying himself
   D. Horatio has not been appropriately rewarded

4. **Why does Pedringano owe Lorenzo a favor?**
   A. Lorenzo once saved his life
   B. Lorenzo found him a mistress
   C. Lorenzo protected him from the Duke's anger before
   D. Lorenzo brought him to the court

5. **What does Lorenzo first promise Pedringano for his services?**
   A. A silver chain
   B. A gold chain
   C. A gold watch
   D. A gold dagger

6. **What is the immediate reason for Pedringano's initial betrayal of Bellimperia?**
   A. Lorenzo offers him a reward
   B. Lorenzo threatens his life
   C. He owes Lorenzo a favor
   D. He despises Bellimperia

7. **How does Pedringano know of Bellimperia's love for Horatio?**
   A. He has heard their amorous conversation
   B. He has seen the two together
   C. He has read her letters
   D. Bellimperia has told him

8. **What does Pedringano promise Lorenzo to do?**
   A. To follow Bellimperia everywhere
   B. To read all of Bellimperia's letters
   C. To murder Horatio
   D. To let Lorenzo know when Horatio and Bellimperia meet

9. **Where do Horatio and Bellimperia plan to meet secretly?**
   A. Horatio's lodging
   B. Hieronimo's bower
   C. In the royal court
   D. Bellimperia's room

10. **When will Horatio meet Bellimperia?**
   A. The same evening
   B. The same afternoon
   C. In three days
   D. Next morning

11. **What will not accompany Bellimperia's marriage to Balthazar?**
   A. A generous gift
   B. A family heirloom
   C. A release from the tribute
   D. A large dowry

12. **Who is supposed to receive Balthazar's ransom?**
   A. The Duke
   B. Horatio
   C. Lorenzo
   D. Hieronimo

13. **Who eventually receives Balthazar's ransom?**
   A. Horatio
   B. Lorenzo
   C. Hieronimo
   D. Pedringano

14. **What does the King entreat the Duke to do?**
   A. Convince Bellimperia to marry Balthazar
   B. Convince Lorenzo to turn Bellimperia in favor of marrying Balthazar
   C. Get rid of Horatio
   D. Go to Portugal to help convince the Viceroy in favor of the marriage

15. **Why does the King desire marriage between Bellimperia and Balthazar?**
   A. He finds Balthazar very attractive
   B. He does not want Horatio to marry Bellimperia
   C. It is politically advantageous
   D. Bellimperia seems to be in love with Balthazar

16. **What does Bellimperia trust Pedringano to do when she meets Horatio in the field?**
   A. Guard the gate
   B. Stay away from the field
   C. Distract Lorenzo and Balthazar
   D. Stay at home

17. **Who is not present when Horatio is murdered?**
   A. Lorenzo's page
   B. Balthazar
   C. Serberine
   D. Pedringano

18. **Where is Horatio hanged?**
   A. In Bellimperia's room
   B. In an arbour
   C. In the woods
   D. From the roof of Hieronimo's house

19. **Who is in disguise when Horatio is murdered?**
   A. Lorenzo
   B. Balthazar
   C. Serberine
   D. Pedringano

20. **Who cries for help when Horatio is murdered?**
   A. Isabella
   B. Serberine
   C. Pedringano
   D. Bellimperia

21. **Why does Hieronimo go looking about in the field at night?**
   A. He could not sleep and wanted to take a walk
   B. He sensed something was wrong
   C. He heard an outcry
   D. He saw shades moving

22. **What does Hieronimo first think when he sees a body hanging in his field?**
   A. That somone has tried to incriminate him
   B. That he must cut down the body
   C. That his son has been murdered
   D. That he must tell his wife

23. **What does Hieronimo vow not to do before exacting revenge for Horatio's death?**
   A. Pray to heaven
   B. Bury the corpse
   C. Mourn for his son
   D. Sleep a wink

24. **What saves Alexandro from his death?**
   A. The Viceroy changes his mind
   B. He convinces the Viceroy of his injustice
   C. The ambassador brings news of Balthazar from spain
   D. Villuppo confesses his crimes

25. **How does Hieronimo first learn of Horatio's murderers?**

A. He has a vision in his dreams

B. Pedringano tells him

C. He overhears Lorenzo in conversation

D. Bellimperia manages to drop him a letter

Quiz 2 Answer Key

1. **(A)** The Duke of Edinburgh
2. **(C)** Hieronimo
3. **(C)** Balthazar is enjoying himself
4. **(C)** Lorenzo protected him from the Duke's anger before
5. **(B)** A gold chain
6. **(B)** Lorenzo threatens his life
7. **(C)** He has read her letters
8. **(D)** To let Lorenzo know when Horatio and Bellimperia meet
9. **(B)** Hieronimo's bower
10. **(A)** The same evening
11. **(B)** A family heirloom
12. **(B)** Horatio
13. **(C)** Hieronimo
14. **(A)** Convince Bellimperia to marry Balthazar
15. **(C)** It is politically advantageous
16. **(A)** Guard the gate
17. **(A)** Lorenzo's page
18. **(B)** In an arbour
19. **(D)** Pedringano
20. **(D)** Bellimperia
21. **(C)** He heard an outcry
22. **(A)** That somone has tried to incriminate him
23. **(B)** Bury the corpse
24. **(C)** The ambassador brings news of Balthazar from spain
25. **(D)** Bellimperia manages to drop him a letter

Quiz 3

1. **What does Bellimperia use to write a letter, for want of ink?**
   A. She sews the message on cloth
   B. Her blood
   C. She carves the message in wood
   D. Tomato juice

2. **What does Lorenzo say when Hieronimo comes looking for Bellimperia?**
   A. The Duke has imprisoned her for a disgrace
   B. He does not know where she is
   C. She is not felling well
   D. She has gone into hiding

3. **Why does Lorenzo ostensibly want to kill Serberine?**
   A. He thinks Serberine stole his gold
   B. He thinks Serberine will betray him
   C. He thinks Serberine has betrayed him
   D. He thinks Serberine is in love with Bellimperia

4. **Where does Pedringano meet Serberine in private?**
   A. Outside his quarters
   B. At Saint Luigi's Park
   C. In Hieronimo's field
   D. In the imperial park

5. **Why are there guards present when Pedringano murders Serberine?**
   A. They happen to be in the area
   B. They have been watching Serberine
   C. They have been following Pedringano
   D. Lorenzo has told them to patrol the area

6. **How does Pedringano kill Serberine?**
   A. He hangs him
   B. He stabs him
   C. He drowns him
   D. He shoots him

7. **Where do the guards take Pedringano?**
   A. To see the King
   B. To see Lorenzo
   C. To see Balthazar
   D. To see Hieronimo

8. **What is Balthazar's reaction to Serberine's death?**
   A. Sorrow
   B. Outrage
   C. Joy
   D. Suspicion

9. **What does Lorenzo send the imprisoned Pedringano?**
   A. A letter
   B. Nothing
   C. A box with a royal pardon
   D. An empty box

10. **What does the page do with the box before handing it over to Pedringano?**
    A. He steals its contents
    B. He opens it
    C. He drops it
    D. He replaces its contents

11. **What does Hieronimo think of Pedringano?**
    A. That he is stupid
    B. That he is a good man
    C. That he is impudent
    D. That he is shy

12. **What does the deputy order the hangman to do with Pedringano's body?**
    A. Throw it in the ocean
    B. Bury it immediately
    C. Leave it unburied
    D. Feed it to the crows

13. **What does the hangman retrieve from Pedringano's body?**
A. A bloody handkerchief
B. A letter addressed to Lorenzo
C. A gold chain
D. A scarf

14. **Who is present when Isabella runs lunatic?**
A. The Duke
B. Her maid
C. Her two servants
D. Hieronimo

15. **Who is Bellimperia's custodian?**
A. Lorenzo
B. Balthazar
C. Pedringano
D. Christophil

16. **What is Lorenzo's excuse for killing Horatio?**
A. He thought Andrea would be fuming in heaven
B. He remembered her old disgrace from her affair with Andrea
C. He disliked Horatio to begin with
D. Balthazar wanted to kill Horatio

17. **Who are the two Portuguese men that Hieronimo meets looking for?**
A. The Duke
B. The King
C. Lorenzo
D. Balthazar

18. **How do the two Portuguese men see Hieronimo?**
A. As a high official
B. As a lowly bastard
C. As a lunatic
D. As an honorable man

19. **Which two objects does Hieronimo have in hand while contemplating suicide?**
    A. A daggard and a halter
    B. A sword and a halter
    C. A daggard and a sword
    D. A halter and a shield

20. **What action does Hieronimo perform in front of the King when asking for justice?**
    A. He points a dagger at Lorenzo
    B. He digs with his dagger
    C. He puts a halter around his neck
    D. He throws a dagger on the ground

21. **What is Lorenzo's explanation for Hieronimo's display of madness in front of the king?**
    A. He has lost his wits in old age
    B. He covets Balthazar's ransom that is due to his son
    C. He is in love with Bellimperia
    D. He is following in Isabella's footsteps

22. **How many citizens come to petition Hieronimo?**
    A. Ten
    B. Two
    C. Four
    D. Three

23. **What is the senex's complaint?**
    A. His tenant refuses to leave
    B. His son has been unjustly murdered
    C. He is owed money
    D. His son has stolen all his money

24. **What does Hieronimo do with the legal papers presented to him?**
    A. He rips them up
    B. He gives them back
    C. He throws them away
    D. He burns them

25. **What does the Viceroy say he would like to do after Balthazar marries Bellimperia?**
    A. Pass on the crown and live a solitary life
    B. Live with Bellimperia
    C. Leave for England
    D. Move to Spain

Quiz 3 Answer Key

1. **(B)** Her blood
2. **(A)** The Duke has imprisoned her for a disgrace
3. **(C)** He thinks Serberine has betrayed him
4. **(B)** At Saint Luigi's Park
5. **(D)** Lorenzo has told them to patrol the area
6. **(D)** He shoots him
7. **(D)** To see Hieronimo
8. **(B)** Outrage
9. **(D)** An empty box
10. **(B)** He opens it
11. **(C)** That he is impudent
12. **(C)** Leave it unburied
13. **(B)** A letter addressed to Lorenzo
14. **(B)** Her maid
15. **(D)** Christophil
16. **(B)** He remembered her old disgrace from her affair with Andrea
17. **(C)** Lorenzo
18. **(C)** As a lunatic
19. **(A)** A daggard and a halter
20. **(B)** He digs with his dagger
21. **(B)** He covets Balthazar's ransom that is due to his son
22. **(D)** Three
23. **(B)** His son has been unjustly murdered
24. **(A)** He rips them up
25. **(A)** Pass on the crown and live a solitary life

Quiz 4

1. **Why is the Duke concerned about the rumors surrounding Lorenzo and Hieronimo?**
   A. It would look bad for Hieronimo to complain to the King about Lorenzo
   B. Hieronimo may challenge Lorenzo to a duel
   C. The Duke fears Hieronimo will prosecute Lorenzo under the law
   D. The Duke is good friends with Hieronimo

2. **What does Bellimperia accuse Hieronimo of?**
   A. Joining league with the Duke
   B. Forgetting her love for Horatio
   C. Forgiving Lorenzo
   D. Neglecting his son's death

3. **What favor do Balthazar and Lorenzo ask of Hieronimo in the fourth act?**
   A. To provide entertainment for the King
   B. To entertain Bellimperia
   C. To welcome the ambassador into his home
   D. To stage the same masque as before

4. **What is the origin of the play that Hieronimo stages?**
   A. Bellimperia found it in the library
   B. Hieronimo bought it in Toledo
   C. Hieronimo wrote it in his youth
   D. Horatio wrote it before his death

5. **What language is not spoken in the play?**
   A. Greek
   B. Latin
   C. Arabic
   D. French

6. **Who is not a character in Hieronimo's play?**
   A. Perseda
   B. Soliman
   C. Selim Calymath
   D. A knight of Rhodes

7. **Who will play the Bashaw?**
   A. Lorenzo
   B. Balthazar
   C. Hieronimo
   D. A page

8. **Who will play Soliman?**
   A. Lorenzo
   B. Balthazar
   C. Hieronimo
   D. Bellimperia

9. **Whose character does Bellimperia's character kill?**
   A. Lorenzo's
   B. Balthazar's
   C. Hieronimo's
   D. No character

10. **What would Balthazar prefer to Hieronimo's tragedy?**
   A. A comedy
   B. A silent masque
   C. A history
   D. An oratorio

11. **Which language will Bellimperia's character speak?**
   A. Italian
   B. Spanish
   C. Latin
   D. French

12. **What does Isabella do before committing suicide?**
   A. She writes Hieronimo a last letter
   B. She cuts down the arbor where Horatio was hung
   C. She cuts up the tables and chairs
   D. She prepares a halter for herself

13. **What does Hieronimo ask the Duke to do before the play begins?**
    A. Toss him the key to the gallery
    B. Read the play to the king
    C. Prepare a special chair for the Viceroy
    D. Disguise himself as a Turk

14. **What does Balthazar bring on stage while Hieronimo and the Duke converse?**
    A. A dagger
    B. A steel chain
    C. A chair
    D. A table

15. **What does Hieronimo note about Balthazar as they prepare for the play?**
    A. His beard is only half-on
    B. He looks nervous
    C. His disguise is crooked
    D. His outfit is magnificent

16. **What aspect of the play does the King remark on?**
    A. Hieronimo's passion
    B. The good acting
    C. The small stage
    D. The fine costumes

17. **What does Hieronimo reveal at the end of the play?**
    A. A bloody handkerchief
    B. His son's corpse
    C. The dead bodies of Lorenzo and Balthazar
    D. Bellimperia's scarf

18. **What does Hieronimo run to do after the play?**
    A. Stab the Duke
    B. Hang himself
    C. Find Isabella
    D. Escape

19. **What does the royal audience demand of Hieronimo?**
   A. His immediate suicide
   B. A written confession for the record
   C. An explanation for the turn of events
   D. An apology

20. **What does Hieronimo do in order to keep his silence?**
   A. He simply says nothing more
   B. He gags himself
   C. He knocks out his teeth
   D. He bites out his tongue

21. **Why is Hieronimo given a knife after he bites out his tongue?**
   A. So that he can sharpen his pen
   B. So that he can reenact Horatio's murder
   C. So that he can stab the Duke
   D. So that he can stab himself

22. **What does the Ghost express at the end of the play?**
   A. Sorrow
   B. Satisfaction
   C. Fury
   D. Frustration

23. **Where will the Ghost lead Bellimperia's soul?**
   A. To rest with himself
   B. To the worst depths of hell
   C. To a place with virgins and queens
   D. To the same place as Horatio

24. **What is in reserve for Pedringano in hell?**
   A. A bed of spikes
   B. A torture rack
   C. Endless flames
   D. Sisyphus's toil

25. **What does Revenge promise for the souls of the villainous characters?**
   A. Slavery under Pluto
   B. No further life in hell
   C. Reincarnation as brutes
   D. An endless tragedy

Quiz 4 Answer Key

1. **(A)** It would look bad for Hieronimo to complain to the King about Lorenzo
2. **(D)** Neglecting his son's death
3. **(A)** To provide entertainment for the King
4. **(C)** Hieronimo wrote it in his youth
5. **(C)** Arabic
6. **(C)** Selim Calymath
7. **(C)** Hieronimo
8. **(B)** Balthazar
9. **(B)** Balthazar's
10. **(A)** A comedy
11. **(D)** French
12. **(B)** She cuts down the arbor where Horatio was hung
13. **(A)** Toss him the key to the gallery
14. **(C)** A chair
15. **(A)** His beard is only half-on
16. **(B)** The good acting
17. **(B)** His son's corpse
18. **(B)** Hang himself
19. **(C)** An explanation for the turn of events
20. **(D)** He bites out his tongue
21. **(A)** So that he can sharpen his pen
22. **(B)** Satisfaction
23. **(C)** To a place with virgins and queens
24. **(C)** Endless flames
25. **(D)** An endless tragedy

ClassicNotes

GradeSaver™

Getting you the grade since 1999™

Other ClassicNotes from GradeSaver™

1984
Absalom, Absalom
Adam Bede
The Adventures of Augie March
The Adventures of Huckleberry Finn
The Adventures of Tom Sawyer
The Aeneid
Agamemnon
The Age of Innocence
Alice in Wonderland
All My Sons
All Quiet on the Western Front
All the King's Men
All the Pretty Horses
The Ambassadors
American Beauty
Angela's Ashes
Animal Farm
Anna Karenina
Antigone
Antony and Cleopatra
Aristotle's Ethics
Aristotle's Poetics
Aristotle's Politics
As I Lay Dying
As You Like It
Astrophil and Stella
The Awakening
Babbitt
The Bacchae
Bartleby the Scrivener
The Bean Trees
The Bell Jar
Beloved
Benito Cereno
Beowulf
Bhagavad-Gita
Billy Budd
Black Boy
Bleak House
The Bloody Chamber
Bluest Eye
The Bonfire of the Vanities
Brave New World
Breakfast at Tiffany's
Call of the Wild
Candide
The Canterbury Tales
Cat's Cradle
Catch-22
The Catcher in the Rye
The Caucasian Chalk Circle
The Cherry Orchard
The Chosen
A Christmas Carol
Chronicle of a Death Foretold
Civil Disobedience
Civilization and Its Discontents
A Clockwork Orange
The Color of Water
The Color Purple
Comedy of Errors
Communist Manifesto
A Confederacy of Dunces
Confessions
Connecticut Yankee in King Arthur's Court
The Consolation of Philosophy
Coriolanus
The Count of Monte Cristo
Crime and Punishment
The Crucible
Cry, the Beloved Country
The Crying of Lot 49
Cymbeline
Daisy Miller
Death in Venice
Death of a Salesman
The Death of Ivan Ilych
Democracy in America
Devil in a Blue Dress
Dharma Bums
The Diary of Anne Frank
Disgrace
Divine Comedy-I: Inferno
A Doll's House
Don Quixote Book I
Don Quixote Book II
Dr. Faustus
Dr. Jekyll and Mr. Hyde
Dracula
Dubliners
East of Eden
Emma

Made in the USA